Contemporary Parks and Gardens in France

Marielle Hucliez

Contemporary Parks and Gardens in France

VILO

PUBLISHING

CONTEMPORARY PARKS AND GARDENS
IN FRANCE

Translation	Rubye Monet

Front Cover
Erik Borja
Corsican garden

Back Cover
Eric Ossart, Arnaud Mairières
La Rizière
Garden Festival, Chaumont-sur-Loire, 1997

Preceding Page
Tobie Loup de Viane
Château de Gourdon, 1972

Editorial Director	Jean-François Gonthier/A.I.E.
Design, layout & cover	Christian Rondet, Françoise Courbis (rondet@easynet.fr)
Editorial Staff	Marielle Hucliez with Clotilde Avenet Olivier Boissière and Sylvie Assassin for the chapter on Jacques Simon
Copyeditor	John H. Liesveld, Jr
Photoengraving	Trio, Sèvres (Hauts-de-Seine)

Copyright © Vilo International, Paris, 2000

ISBN : 2-84576-006-X
Printed in the European Community

VILO INTERNATIONAL - 30, rue de Charonne - F75011 Paris

Contents

Parks, Gardens and Landscapes

Painters, designers, architects, entomologists, doctors, agronomists, botanists and all manner of self-taught people have felt an attraction to gardens and, in the course of a journey that is emotional and aesthetic, philosophical and social, have yielded to the temptations of the landscape. Gardener? Landscape architect? The complex blend of knowledge and skills that make up this art are reflected in the very names (past and present) that have been given to its practitioners: landscape architect, horticultural engineer, town planning engineer, landscape artist... The field of their endeavors extends from the restoration of historic gardens to the creation of city parks, from the rehabilitation of the inner city to the rectification of the outlying areas. Their domain stretches from town to country, embracing the outskirts and connective links, the roads, seashores and riverbanks, active zones and abandoned territories.

The increasing attention paid to landscape over the past 20 years, both to the remarkable landscapes of our heritage and to the ordinary landscapes of our everyday life, results from (and is sustained by) commissions from the public sector. This appropriation of common space has been accompanied by reflection and debate about our times, our society and its problems.

Louis Benech, private garden in Touraine, 1988.

Opposite page:
Yves Brunier, with Jean Nouvel, Autoroute du Sud, 1988.

Jacqueline Osty,
Saint-Pierre Park,
Amiens, 1994.

Bernard Lassus,
Jardin des Retours,
La Corderie Royale park,
Rochefort, 1991.

Parks, Gardens and Landscapes

"When the universe expands, landscape returns," writes Michel Serres in *The Five Senses*. In July, 1969, the vision of the earth as seen from the moon hit humanity with the force of a revelation: the astronauts who had escaped the earth's gravity discovered with new eyes the beauty of the planet, its forests, deserts and icy poles, its vast oceans stretched like watery plains between the relief of the continents. Navigators of space, they observed the stars and dreamed of the shore. When they returned their first words were for the earth—could it be they were afraid of not finding it again?

This vision of splendor and vulnerability certainly went far to trigger an increased awareness about the environment and secretly stimulated all those who were concerned in its conservation—by protection as well as by innovation.

In 1975 the French government set up the Conservatoire du Littoral (shoreline conservation authority). In 1981 it drew up a pre-inventory of several regions, which later resulted in a systematic inventory, covering all of France, of "gardens of historic, botanical or scenic interest."

The discovery of just how many "outstanding gardens" actually existed came as a surprise, even to their owners. The first "Visit a French Garden" campaign was launched in June 1989, with the aim of making better known the public heritage but also (and this was the great novelty) the private heritage.

In 1991 Michel Racine, in his *Guide des jardins de France,* listed 550 gardens open to the public, selected for their scenic and botanical quality. This inventory stems not from any obsession with conservation, but reflects rather a new awareness of recent creation, notably in public parks. In *Jardins de France,* published in 1997, he presents 750 outstanding gardens, and writes: *"This guide reveals the full scope of the phenomenon. In the past five years over 200 gardens have offered visitors a new experience, either because they have recently been reopened, or have undergone extensive renovation or are entirely new creations. At a time when all our points of reference—historic, scientific, definition of territory or notions of modernity—have exploded in every direction, France has witnessed a multitude of initiatives (...) with a proliferation of ideas, reflecting the diversity of the various gardeners."*

There, the word is out of the bag—"gardener." Some of the leading French landscape architects of today have proudly reclaimed the term and are living up to its responsibilities.

The reality and fragility of the plant world raise, from the outset (before even thinking about questions of maintenance), problems inherent in planting and growth. This essential relation between time and duration is at the root of much intraprofessional bickering in regard to the position of the architect and that of the landscaper. The architect conceives and constructs in such a way as to resist the wear and tear of time. The landscaper, who handles living material, works with and within time. Aside from the changing of the season, the perception of a garden depends largely on its evolution and growth, on the delicate balance between the parts and the whole, and on a complex series of adaptations, transmutations and the integration of "accidents..."

Visiting a garden with the person who cares for it and assures its survival, reading a landscape with someone who has modeled it, strolling through city streets and squares with the one who has defined their look and provided a key for their perception, and listening to the creators of gardens and landscapes talk about their approach, practice and philosophy—this is the most vivid way to grasp the diversity of contemporary approaches and to have a long look, both pleasurable and instructive, at the landscape.

009

The renewal of interest in landscape and gardening arts marks the end of a long eclipse. Following the bold urban planning schemes of Haussmann in the last century, which annexed the grandiose parks of Paris—the Bois de Boulogne, Bois de Vincennes, or Buttes Chaumont—the French tradition seemed to have been lost. The only ones who kept the art quietly alive were a few rich amateurs like Albert Kahn or Edith Wharton, for whom gardening was a beloved pastime. In the 1920's and 1930's the architects of "heroic modernity," fascinated by the industrial revolution, were not much attracted by a nature abstractly treated in plan and poorly carried out in reality. The natural setting of architecture and of the town was left, so to speak, to its own devices. The fact that the "Cubist garden" created by Gabriel Guévrékian for the villa of Marie-Laure and Charles de Noailles in Hyères on the French Riviera (actually no more than a modest, if colorful, triangle), attracted such attention shows how exceptional an event it must have been.

After the war came the urgent need for reconstruction, and the near fatal errors committed later came to be excused by "extenuating circumstances." The vast tracts of public housing with their chlorphylled interstices clearly show the attitude of disdain that prevailed at that time. This was the dawn of national planning in France and the reorganization of land in provincial regions into what some referred to as "the capitalist kolkhoz." As for the main infrastructures—highways, bridges and viaducts, high tension lines, dams and railroads, they were the monopoly of engineers and technocrats.

With the apotheosis of growth and the reign of consumer society, a sneaking suspicion was born that perhaps nature had been too quickly excluded from the domain of progress and might have its role to play after all. The new attitudes of the 1960's exploded in France into May '68 and marked a turning point for society at large. The "children of Marx and Coca-Cola" along with their taste for grass (of various sorts) and their dreams of changing the world, also yearned for a return to nature and the joys of bucolic life. Yet the planners were still totally focused on urban concerns.

Garden arts were to make their re-entry through architecture, the very discipline that had once pushed them out. Mainly, though not exclusively, it was the members of the Atelier d'Urbanisme et Architecture (AUA), convinced of the social role of the architect, who were responsible for the return to preoccupations with landscape. Architects like Loiseau, Tribel, Deroche, Chemetov, Ciriani and Huidobro coopted Corajoud, Simon, Vexlard, Chemetoff, Grunig, Tribel and later Clément. The beginnings were timid and, in retrospect, the designs of the 1970's seem a bit stiff and overly functional—concrete roadways with concrete rest areas. But the aim was not to prettify. Their first concern was durability and ease of maintenance. The movement soon spread. The dropouts of May '68, who suspected architecture and design of collusion with the capitalists and the consumer society, fled their traditional art schools, Beaux-Arts or Arts-Décoratifs, and signed up instead at the Versailles Horticultural School which, under their impulse, was to transform itself into the "Landscape School" in 1973. There, the pioneers found their disciples. Aside from learning the necessary skills, they began to lay the theoretical foundation for their profession. They quickly enrolled history in its service—undoubtedly significant in this respect was the presence just nearby of the most famous garden of all time, designed by Le Nôtre for Louis XIV at the Versailles Palace. Just as the training of an architect is imbued with the history of the town and its strata, so the study of the land and its divisions nourishes the reflection of French landscape architects and plays a key role in their practice.

The diversity of landscaping needs grew at the same time as a body of specialists was being formed and a fully-fledged discipline being born. French landscape architecture, though sometimes called a school, is really a nebula of indistinct shape. The public commissions that marked its beginnings are no longer limited to providing facelifts for the low-rent housing projects that served as its first alibi. In the 1980's, the powers-that-be had discovered that architecture could serve as a visual support for their public image and allow them to leave their mark in history, a praiseworthy ambition, though not without electoral considerations. Eventually they realized that landscaping is another means of communication, even more virtuous than the first. For who would dare be against nature? The only catch was that you had to give it time to grow. Given the success of fast food, who knows if there may be a future for "speed-gardening"?

The domain open to French landscape architects is nevertheless vast. Old or historic gardens are rehabilitated, new private gardens flourish, parks and squares, green malls and avenues multiply in urban settings, while flowered traffic circles punctuate provincial intersections... On the national level, the public authorities are beginning to assert themselves: highway contractors, after a period of planting roadsides with questionable works of art, have begun to adopt more subtle strategies; the venerable SNCF, the French state railroad company, perhaps due to prodding by ecology groups, is taking a hard look at its old infrastructures; and the EDF, the electricity company, is redesigning its pylons and burying its lines... But the questions raised by territorial planning are different, and more serious; the reclamation of abandoned industrial sites, whose proximity to towns make it an immediate necessity, has begun here and there in the hard-hit industrial areas of the Nord and Lorraine, with the aid of seasoned professionals like Jacques Sgard or Bertrand Folléa. As for unused agricultural lands, they pose the immense problem of what to do with them: is reconversion for tourism the only solution?

After a phase of convalescence, in which it took a slightly moralizing stance, the discipline has now gained in conceptual liberty and enlarged its vision. The media hype around Gilles Clément and his "global garden" is revealing in this respect. Is it the timidity of the authorities or their unswerving attachment to French tradition? The thrill of exuberant modernity, a taste of which was brought by the work of the late and much missed Yves Brunier, is not yet perceptible. Will salvation come from the land artists or from that fabulous laboratory of the imagination, the Garden Festival, held every year at Chaumont-sur-Loire?

This book offers a broad panorama of French landscape practice today. Far from exhaustive, its modest aim is to arouse the curiosity of garden admirers and casual observers alike, and to bear witness to a welcome evolution. May this be only the beginning!

The Sausset Park (started 1979),
first major project of Michel and
Claire Corajoud, spreads over 200
hectares between the exurban
areas north of Paris and the broad
stretches of farmland that
surround Charles de Gaulle Airport.
It is bordered by the motorway
A1, crossed by a highway and a
suburban train line, and marked
by constructions such as high
tension lines and water towers.

Michel & Claire Corajoud

Giving a lecture to the students in his landscape class, Michel Corajoud exclaims: *"What you've got to have is visual bulimia... At the start of a project, give priority to effervescence. Explore the site in every direction. Multiply your points of view. Every spot is full of promise..."* Ubiquity of the senses, a will to surpass the mere object and a constant opening toward the horizon are some of the characteristic traits of this unusual and complex figure, whose influence marked a whole generation of landscape designers.

A graduate of the school of Arts Décoratifs, Corajoud was early on associated with the AUA architects Enrique Ciriani and Borja Huidobro, who were working to profoundly change public housing. A decisive encounter with Jacques Simon, who at the same time was focusing public attention on the way of looking at landscape, also influenced a way of thinking that Corajoud was to refine over his years of teaching. At Versailles he was one of the key figures responsible for transforming the Ecole Nationale d'Horticulture into the Ecole Nationale Supérieure du Paysage de Versailles.

> *"Our future seems to me more linked to an effort of recomposing the territory and repairing the blighted suburbs, than to the somewhat artificial restoration of the idea of a garden. What I know about gardens is that they were the place of choice where a given society expressed its certainties and affirmed its coherence. I don't think we live today in that kind of a society. And if we did, I'm not sure I'd want to be among those who express it."*

In his teaching as in his practice, Corajoud concentrated on public space, thus on the city in its relation to nature. The Sausset Park, which he has worked on for 20 years with his partner (in private as well as professional life) Claire Corajoud, illustrates the working concepts that are the foundation of his art: a constant awareness of time through the use of plants—like trees—that endlessly "retard" and modify the project; an integration of objects that punctuate and dramatize the landscape—motorways, high tension lines, railroads, buildings, bridges and tunnels; and lastly, the importance he gives to the horizon, which affords an escape from the cramped dimensions of the city.

> *"When I am working with a given space, what interests me most is its relation to other spaces around it. That is what I call the horizon, the way in which each space impinges on the neighboring one, which in turn unfolds into another one, gradually reaching what we call the horizon.*
>
> *"There is no space without a horizon. And beyond that horizon which frames the landscape, there is another landscape to discover. The horizon, that line where earth touches sky, is one more landscape to cross, one that liberates us from confinement."*

Embankments planted
with windbreaks to protect
the young trees and aid their
rapid growth, speeding up the
density of the vegetation.

Michel & Claire Corajoud

In 1979 the General Council of the Seine-Saint-Denis department, in the northern suburbs of Paris, opened a competition for the creation of a 200-hectare park on a tract of agricultural land adjacent to the towns of Aulnay-sous-Bois, Villepinte and Saint-Denis. The idea was to create a space open to all in a natural, that is, primarily vegetal setting. At first glance it was a bare flat site marked by high tension wires, water towers, highways, a railroad line and a suburban train station.

Creating a park of this size on the outskirts of Paris—even though it was smaller than its venerable predecessors, the Bois de Vincennes and the Bois de Boulogne—was still a major event. The leading names of the day in landscape design took part: among them Alain Provost, Alexandre Chemetoff, Jacques Sgard and Gilles Vexlard, as well as Jacques Coulon and the winners Claire and Michel Corajoud.

Rebirth of a forest on bare stretches that were once farmland. After 19 years, the view from the water towers embraces the plateau on which dense forest allées define a landscape dotted with clearings and crisscrossed by intersecting pathways, according to traditional forest layout in France.

This territory bordering the towns and opening onto the plain was not without natural assets: it had fertile soil and water in the form of two streams, the Sausset and the Roideau, and Savigny Lake. A distinctive feature of the winning design consisted of replacing the usual retaining pool with a marsh to protect against a sudden rise in water in case of storm. Jacques Coulon, who had come up with a similar idea, was associated with the two winners for the first phase of the park.

The first plantings were done on the park's periphery, so as to clearly mark its boundaries and to discourage any future attempts to encroach on the territory by ill-considered development. New plastic mulching techniques allowed for rapid growth of young trees. In the park proper, traditional forestry techniques were used to arrange familiar forms as they are found in the surroundings: crossroads and clearings, groves and hedgerows.

015

Michel & Claire Corajoud

Around the Sausset stream that gives the park its name, Corajoud gave free rein to a landscape of hedgerows.

Between the park and surrounding residential areas, the pathways created by the landscape architects followed the natural paths made by the residents.

Michel & Claire Corajoud

Another priority was to create pathways between different areas, in particular to and from the train station, including tunnels or overpasses for roads and railroad.

From the station, the landscape architects organized different "scenes": a forest scene on the plateau, which would join up with Aulnay-sous-Bois Park; a scene of trees and farmland to go with the planned ecomuseum; a bocage scene opening southward toward the new town of Villepinte; and a more urban scene near the new Aulnay 3000 development and around the Savigny basin.

On the shores of Lake Savigny, a promenade made of wooden footbridges punctuated by small belvederes.

Today, 16 years after the first plantings, the Sausset Park is a work in progress: the young plants that measured only 30 centimeters have become vigorous young trees. The work, which has progressed step by step since 1981, is still going on and the park is taking shape in its promised form.

Michel & Claire Corajoud

A slightly undulating stairway
crosses the prairie and leads to
the wide footbridge over the
RER line.

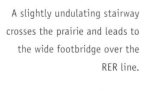

Michel & Claire Corajoud

On the outskirts of town, an "urban" park makes the transition with the forest landscape. A geometric structure governs planted spaces of one hectare each.

019

Michel & Claire Corajoud

Michel & Claire Corajoud

Opposite page:
A rustic wooden footbridge crosses an arm of Lake Savigny, whose shore is lined with promenades and dotted with benches.

Water towers and pylons of high-tension lines form an integral part of the landscape. They are powerful landmarks, visible from Lake Savigny on the south, and mark the boundaries of the horizon.

Michel & Claire Corajoud

Alexandre Chemetoff's
Bureau des Paysages, is part
and parcel of the configuration
of the Paris inner suburbs, with
dividing walls and the remains
of a former orchard.

Alexandre Chemetoff

"I am a landscape architect. That doesn't mean I compose landscapes. To me, landscaping implies discipline and meeting the exigencies of the project. I see it as a way of building and developing." In this way Alexandre Chemetoff defines a profession and a practice that for him are linked with his close connections to architecture. "If I were to sum up the high points of my training, I would cite my visits to building sites with my father Paul Chemetov, my meeting with Michel Corajoud, and my relations with Michel Corajoud and Jacques Simon."

In 1979, having just graduated from the Ecole nationale supérieure du paysage de Versailles, Chemetoff entered the major competition of the moment, that of Sausset Park, then the one for La Villette. In 1985, Bernard Tschumi, the project manager for La Villette, invited him to participate in the project, to create a theme garden that would be called "Le Jardin de l'Energie." Chemetoff began with a general reflection on the project and a questioning on the meaning of the "gardening arts" at the end of our century. He then decided to install within the sequence that forms the core of the park a hollow space, where a botanical species, bamboo, would vie with a product of human ingenuity, concrete. The final result, which came to be known as the Bamboo Garden, is a place of trial and error, of expression, production and rebirth, where horticultural skill and technical know-how cohabit and confront each other. "The bamboo garden is a place I love. It represents my ideal—like a manifesto in foliage and concrete. My itinerary as a city gardener has taught me to love concrete, not when it is polished or architectonic, but rough and crude like in some admirable works of civil engineering."

The urban projects that Chemetoff has worked on in recent years are either those of repair ("designing small areas of urban tissue" in crowded suburban sites) of development (banks of the Vilaine River in Rennes) or else landscaping work on spaces bordering new constructions (a public

Alexandre Chemetoff

Opposite page:

A rectilinear path
withalternating stripes
of black and white stones,
the signature of Daniel Buren
in the Bamboo Garden.

A concrete wall forms
the retaining wall of the garden
and helps to create a micro-
climate adapted to the plantings.

park at La Courneuve, an urban development zone and a water garden in Nancy). They all show a determination that a public space should be *"a place of exchange and sharing, an area that should mediate between a multitude of private interests and the general interest."*

This idea of shared landscape, belonging to no one and to everyone at the same time, has governed the development of the beach front at Le Havre, a project aimed at opening the town to its estuary and the sea. *"It's all about rediscovering horizons, walking to the edge of town... a series of emotions, ordinary and nearly indiscernible, so much does the place resemble others, yet all the while keeping its own identity."*

If some artists seek to mark their works with the stamp of originality, Alexandre Chemetoff makes a virtue of "radical banality." Not in renunciation, but in the conquest of a precious value. The condition for this conquest lies in an increased attention paid to territory and landscape, through rereading the history of the place and rediscovering its geography... *"What use is the landscape? The geographer Yves Lacoste once answered that its use is to make war. I say its use is to order and plan the land, thus, to make peace."*

Bamboo Garden, La Villette, Paris

The Bamboo Garden designed by Alexandre Chemetoff is a sort of "climatic theater" specially created to shelter new species. Beneath its apparent uniformity, bamboo is really extremely diverse. Visitors are invited to test the acuity of their perception on the minuscule differences between the 30 varieties that make up this remarkable collection.

It is a medium-sized garden, 3,000 square meters as compared with the 35 hectares of the entire park. It is a space in three dimensions, hollowed out of the ground, in a site with a long history. This excavation, five meters deep, creates the micro-climate favorable for the growth of bamboo.

The digging uncovered a host of drainage networks and technical galleries, which had once served the stockyards and slaughterhouses that formerly occupied this site. Chemetoff took the constraint and turned it to his advantage, making it a forceful element of the project. Choosing to show what is usually hidden, he used the canalizations to fashion the landscape. By a similar logic, the need to evacuate water retained on the garden floor is used as an opportunity to install a series of fountains.

Two artists were invited to take part in the project. Bernhard Leitner conceived an architecture of sounds by using the walls, embankments and bamboo plantings as a music chamber. The "sound cylinder" placed in the hollow of the garden evokes a machine for suspending time. Is it the sound of wind, leaves, or water that the cylinder captures and reproduces in the manner of an echo chamber? Daniel Buren introduced a discreet and abstract order, both geometric and arithmetic, thanks to simple black and white bands running the entire length of the installation.

Alexandre Chemetoff has a favorite itinerary for exploring the space: *"I like to enter by the water stairway and go down to the sound cylinder. The noise of the city fades away, slowly replaced by the murmur of running water. When you reach a precise spot at the bottom of the stairs, you know you are in the garden... I follow the paths, then leave by the curved stairway. When I laid it out I imagined a sort of jungle trail hacked out through the bamboo. It took the form of a curve, haphazard, but with an assurance based on the trace of repeated passages. It is not a path we are following, but rather the steps of those who went before."*

The entrance to Bernhard Leitner's "sound cylinder" is flanked by two moucharabias, in the center of which a vertical channel guides the flow of drainage water.

Footpaths and canalizations cross the sunken space of the garden and mingle with the bamboo.

026

The red metal "Follies," "deconstruction" structures by Bernard Tschumi, are scattered throughout the park and serve as landmarks.

Alexandre Chemetoff

Alexandre Chemetoff

Opposite page:

Following the hills of Sainte-Adresse, the beach in Le Havre stretches along the Channel coast. The scene inspired paintings by Monet and other impressionists, as well as their forerunner, Eugene Boudin.

After the summer season, when the beach is empty, the containers that hold all the equipment vanish and the area becomes once again a place for strolling.

From the diluted waters of the Seine estuary to the sea-front of the English Channel, the Le Havre beach lies between the port where the great steamships used to dock and the hills of Sainte-Adresse. Today, tankers and freighters pass less than two miles away.

Chemetoff began to work *"starting from the strong points the site already had"* to recreate the conditions that would give the city back its beach and seascape.

To bring the inhabitants closer to a sea that was for too long distanced by a broad shore, he established a series of lines parallel to the landscape, in successive strata that lead the walker from the asphalt of the boulevard to the pebbles of the beach.

To attenuate the noise of the boulevard, he built a sunken pedestrian walkway. The aquatic garden and its fresh-water stream, whose source is the foot of the Sainte-Adresse hills, enable the plantings to better resist the aggressions of the salt spray from the sea. A gentle dune, a sloping prairie and a dike built 100 meters from the high tide line mark the progression toward the sea. Aluminum-covered containers (reflecting the colors of the sky) hold all the necessary amenities of summer life on the beach—bathing huts, seasonal food stands and lookout posts. *"I wanted to give the beach a character that varied with the seasons. In summer, it's a lively, bustling little town. In winter it recovers its empty sea-front atmosphere."*

For three long years, a succession of workers, from road-pavers to gardeners, took turns plying their skills. *"I'd like to think that visitors don't quite see the changes, that they have the feeling that the beach is neither just the same nor completely different, but as it always was in their reminiscences."*

"Now, just outside Le Havre, we have a little summer seaside town, at the brink of the water and the edge of town, where you can contemplate the city as you stroll along the sea. As you do so, you may come to realize that what was missing from the architecture of Perret (who rebuilt Le Havre after the war) was not pergolas nor flower beds in front of the town hall, but an opening of the city toward the sea."

Alexandre Chemetoff

The footpath and the aquatic
garden with its brook, fed by
a spring tapped at the foot of the
hill, create an ample transition
between the boulevard and
the beach. From the architecture
of the sea front to the sand
on the shore, a series of bands
with precise functions alternate
nature and artifice.

Alexandre Chemetoff

Alexandre Chemetoff

The winter quiet of the shore
alternates with the busy hum
of bustling summer activity, with
a range of seasonal constructions.

The prairie and the restaurants...
so many elements have helped
win back the inhabitants
of Le Havre who for many years
had ignored their beach.

Alexandre Chemetoff

Alexandre Chemetoff

Jacques Coulon

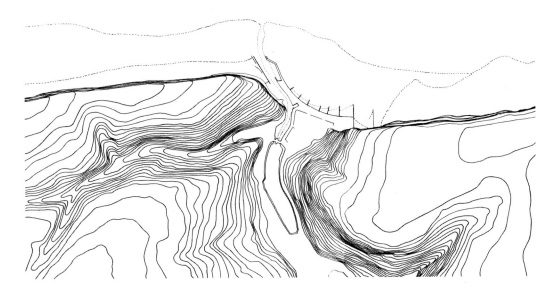

The chalk cliffs sculpted by the sea and the resulting projection of loose pebbles create a topographic situation typical of this part of the Channel coast.

It was May 1968 that made Jacques Coulon abandon the Ecole des Arts Décoratifs, where he had just been admitted, and turn his attention to landscaping. It was autumn of 1968, just three weeks after the start of term, when he quit the Ecole des Arts Décoratifs to enter the Landscape Department of the Versailles Ecole d'Horticulture.

There he studied the history of gardens but found no continuity therein with which he could comfortably identify. Instead, he chose to plunge headlong into the times, coming to grips with its architecture and the problems posed by urbanization.

In 1979 he came in third in the competition for the Sausset Park, in the Seine-Saint-Denis department. His conception was close to that of the winning team, Michel and Claire Corajoud, with whom he participated on the first phase of the project.

His prime aim was to seek efficient answers to all the precise questions raised by landscape management (facilities, waste treatment stations, motorway access roads, recreation parks, etc.). With this in mind, he would regularly choose modest, well-ordered projects that allowed for practice and experimentation.

Today he takes on more open projects, on a larger scale in time and space. He has worked on the development of the banks of the Marne, on the university campus of Orleans and as well as advisor to the Ministry of Planning and Development for the Côtes-d'Armor Department.

Opposite page:
The promenade by Jacques Coulon and the architect Rémy Lacau at the entrance to the beach of Saint-Valéry-en-Caux, a balcony on the sea and a rampart protecting the town.

Jacques Coulon

In 1988 Jacques Coulon won the competition along with the architect Rémy Lacau for a project to connect the little town of Saint-Valéry-en-Caux with its seafront.

The beach of Saint-Valéry-en-Caux is framed by two chalk cliffs over 60 meters high. This dramatic geographic setting already provides an exceptional setting. But the constraints of the project are nonetheless exceptional. The site is so oriented on the English Channel that the violence of wind and sea flings pebbles from the beach right up onto the promenades. To combat this, Coulon took two types of measures. Facing the sea, within protection already in place—sea wall, jetties and breakwaters—he restructured the promenades, creating higher and lower ones, corresponding to tide levels. Facing south, away from the sea, he installed spaces for activities protected from the wind: covered sand beaches, wooden terraces, pools for children. No planting was possible in the salt spray, but great care was taken in the choice of materials and in the layout, which follows the movement of the sea.

"Coming from the center of town, you suddenly discover the coast, with the cliffs and the sea, and the emotion is a strong one (...) Since all is revealed at first sight, the promenade has no possible progression, it can only repeat itself. (...) As people stroll back and forth, chatting as they walk,

we want the views to be varied and multiple. There is a lower promenade that follows the general curve of the old sea wall and gives on the pebble beach, which is invaded at the slightest storm. Other paths branch off and take refuge behind slightly inclined walls, forming second or third ramparts of protection. These successive lines reveal the basic contradiction of the situation; we come here for a confrontation with the elements, to see and feel the sea, the wind, the spray and yet at the same time we seek protection from them. A movement to, yet away... we approach with our backs turned. In a word, that is the project."

037

Opposite page:

Set between two cliffs more than 60 meters high, the seafront lies in a harsh mineral setting.

The promenades, with their long, low walls and zigzag forms, overlook the pebble beach.

Jacques Coulon

Against the assault of sea
and pebbles, Coulon set up
a series of successive defenses
that shelter strollers, even during
high tides of the equinox.

Jacques Coulon

Well-protected by dikes
and distinct from the paths,
the facilities reproduce those
of a traditional beach: sand,
solarium and freshwater pools
sheltered from the wind.

Jacques Coulon

Between 1960 and 1975 Jacques Simon devoted nearly all his efforts to public housing projects. Here, the Urban Development Zone (ZUP) of Chatillons (Reims, 1970). Undulations made by bulldozers directly on the building site rubble, covered with grass, then planted with saplings.The flowing sensual curves give a strong visual and tactile pleasure, all the more striking for the brutal and monolithic rationalism that serves as a setting.

Jacques Simon

Today landscape is in the limelight. The present infatuation tends to make us forget the long eclipse in the middle of the century and the reasons for it. In the 1960's and 1970's technology ruled the development of urban space, reducing everything to abstract and measurable entities. All that was expected of a landscape architect was to provide a vegetal accompaniment to architecture. Jacques Simon had anticipated the essential role that landscape would be called upon to play in contemporary society. He was one of the main instigators of the mutation. Using a language of great sobriety, he gave back to landscaping a dimension of sensitivity, stamped with social preoccupations.

Simon has more than one string to his bow. Writing has long been an essential activity. He signed his first publications in 1960 when he was barely out of the Versailles Ecole d'Horticulture. These were followed by books and innumerable articles. Wishing to preserve his freedom of expression, he took over and directed the review *Espaces Verts* and created an independent publishing house that printed more than 20 of his works. These publications were to play a significant role. It was after reading one of these articles that Ian McHarg invited him to teach in Philadelphia in 1960 and that Paul Chemetov persuaded him to join for a time the AUA. Their affinities stemmed from a similar critical approach to the rule of science and the Cartesian spirit that dominated Western thought. For American landscape architects, the struggle was against a social structure that imprisoned and threatened man by upsetting the environment.

For the members of AUA, it was against the dominance of business and a push toward productivity that ruled town planning in the period 1960-70.

For Simon, practice, teaching and writing are inseparable. With pen — or rather felt-tipped marker — in hand, he makes use of the word as well as the image, wielding both with speed and precision, bolstered by a wealth of knowledge and a virtuosity forged over the years. A man of broad culture, nourished on the writings of Thoreau, Ian McHarg, Ian Nairn, Sylvia Crowe, Gordon Cullen, to mention but a few, Jacques Simon is also an indefatigable traveler, for whom a direct confrontation with the reality of the terrain is at the heart of his work. The United States, Canada and Northern Europe have attracted him in particular, but Southern Europe, the Orient and Africa have also been included in his interminable odyssey.

Jacques Simon, right, with farmer Claude Hugot, at the start of planting for the "Flag of Europe" (Turny, Burgundy, 1990).

The first to receive the Grand Prix du Paysage in 1990, he owes this official recognition to a number of new ideas that have strongly influenced the French scene, although he has never limited his concerns to his own country, but rather sought a living confrontation with foreign experiences.

Ephemeral landscape works created in 1996, at Turny (Yonne).

Below: *Mouvements* (straw added to a burnt field).

Opposite, above: *Pantomime* (burnt straw).

Below: *Soleil* (colza in flower).

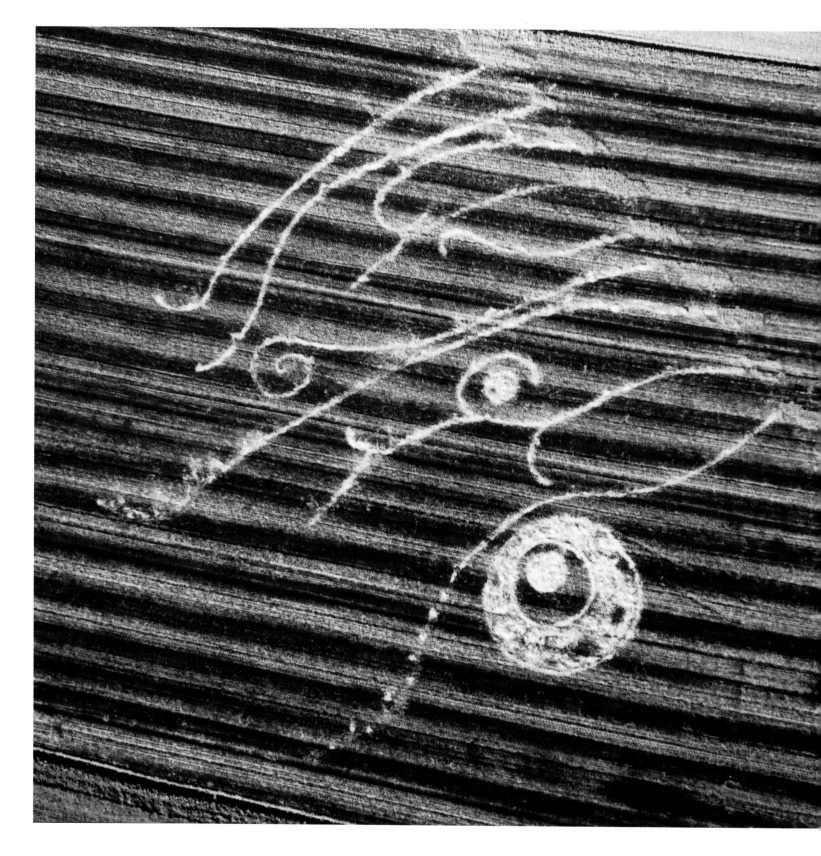

Jacques Simon

His ephemeral landscape creations, messages or drawings with the earth for a canvas, which are shot by aerial photography then vanish with the cycle of the seasons, reveal a duality of discovery and disappearance. Fragile, tactile and mobile—the underlying influence of American culture is undeniable. As for his landscape design, it is an open process, an empathy with a place. The inspiration comes from an emotional reaction to the context, rather than from a patient intellectual construction. *"The landscape designer must have a sort of seventh sense for nature and the ecological element inherent in it. He must seek to identify himself with that nature. To refuse the decorative, to seek simplicity and economy, is at the root of the conception. The landscape is expressed through the shape of the earth itself, a sculpture in land that is then clothed with trees."*

043

Jacques Simon

La Fôret flottante
glides along the Seine...,
with artist Lynn Chargueraud
and Ludovic Bednar, Paris 1992.

Dérive,
with Lynn Chargueraud,
landscape designer
Eric François, and
Erwan Simon, Paris 1989.

Jacques Simon

Fascinated by the city, convinced of the social role of landscape, Simon has devoted a great part of his activity to urban peripheries. One of his essential contributions to zones of urban development (Nangis, Provins, Reims—the site of the famous Saint-John Perse Park) and a new town, Le Vaudreuil, is to have treated the vegetal element as a volume. The density of the planting reinforces the legibility of the spaces by creating visual lines and perspectives. In a space poor in impressions, Simon creates surprise effects, arouses emotions, calls up intense images that imprint the memory and generate order and landmarks that counterbalance the disorientation characteristic of these hybrid spaces of the Athens Charter.

In more recent times, the "methodology of emergency" that had become the mark of the landscape architect has given way to a more measured approach, dealing with preoccupations Simon has always been concerned with—destruction of the environment, the fragile balance of biotopes, the hegemony of the automobile, and the great changes of rural society...

Simon's attitudes show a true modernity of thought: he bridges disciplines and takes on different roles. The elasticity of frontiers, interrelation of genres, search for transversality in a world governed by overly rigid structures, all notions for which his work openly pleads, find a broad echo in young contemporary creators.

Jacques Simon

Jacques Simon

This project, situated in the Jura Department, is currently being realized in collaboration with the research division of the motorway agency Scetauroute. It consists of the reconversion of a quarrying zone (used for the construction of Motorway A 39) into a recreational area.

Once the sand quarry had ceased operations, its edges were spontaneously replenished, and the first step was to protect them from any project that might have a harmful effect.

The vocation of the site was to combine education and recreation, including initiation to environment, relaxation, leisure activities and various gatherings. The key word was economy—in costs as well as in means. The pond, covering 60 hectares, was irregular in shape, its winding contours forming deep coves along the wooded banks. This aimed at increasing the available area and making it possible to separate different activities and create zones of tranquility, propitious to plant and animal diversity.

Thanks to the contour of the site, the moderately rolling relief, and the great variety of forest-type planting, the visitor can enjoy a range of visions, both distant and close.

The photo shows the state of the site before the project; the drawings show the effect after several years. The plant composition attests to the biological quality of the former sand quarries. Additional species were added with a view to enriching the biotope.

047

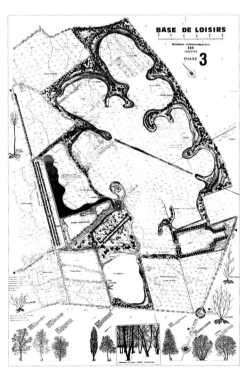

Jacques Simon

Jacques Simon

"The motorway is a line that refuses the environment." The truth of this statement is often reinforced by the insipid plant accompaniment or overuse of concrete, the all too frequent solutions used with motorways.

To offset the "trench effect" and link up the roadside with what already exists, the two favorite tools of the landscape architect are embankments and vegetation. In this way he creates movement and a powerful visual rhythm that breaks the monotony of the drive, while at the same time opening vistas to the distance.

In the rest area of Crocs-de-la-Terre at Villechétif (1991), near Troyes (created with Damery-Vetter-Weil and Domique Perset, architects) three mounds of earth rise to a height of over 12 meters, each bordered on its crest by a strip of young trees that annually heightens the existing volume.

The surface area of motorway rest stops has considerably increased over the years. Rarely over five hectares in 1970, they are often four times as large nowadays, thus providing a large amount of usable landfill.

At Villeroy (1997), a rest area situated to the west of Sens (project built with Denis Sloan, architect), the four mounds, 70 meters long, topped by a curved line of a local variety of trees, make it possible not to take in the entire site at one glance.

Aerial view of Villechétif.

The mounds of Villechétif and Villeroy, from the earthworks to finishing touches. The rhythm of the seasons plays with that of the volumes. In summer, the branches of the saplings (willows below, hornbeam at the top) reach to the ground so that the trees add height to the hills.

Jacques Simon

The landscape improvement project (1994) of this 1930's housing development accompanied the renovation and densification of the neighborhood. To counterbalance the strong presence of cars on the Avenue Charles-de-Gaulle, the original concept was to create, parallel to the main thoroughfare, a sort of valley within the built-up space.

Although the project never actually materialized, the idea of an alternate itinerary was kept, visually marked by rocks and boulders and linking the Henri-Sellier Park to a future park, to be designed by Jacqueline Osty.

The inner courtyards between buildings were occupied by family gardens. The new treatment seeks to impose a somewhat public status to these spots, while preserving the ensemble of private gardens. Curved lines replaced the square layout of the old kitchen gardens, in a system close to that used by the Danish landscapist Sorenson—household gardens are inserted in ovals surrounded by hedges between which pedestrians can stroll. To accompany these undulations, the ground is also marked by gentle curves.

Here and there, the space is punctuated by references to the neighborhood's past, like the hedges in the passages between the buildings or the small white wooden doors that were imitated for the newly built entrances.

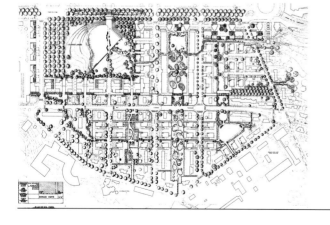

Jacques Simon

For the Ile Saint-Denis Park (1984) a plan of earthworks, followed by another of planting, were conceived by the landscape architect and implemented by the parks department of the municipality, which will also be responsible for its future upkeep.

The island, long used to hold landfill, was encumbered by a large volume of earth, to which Simon added another 300,000 square meters to model the terrain, increasing the available area and creating variety. The landscaping respects the initial feeling of the site. Thus, the intimate quality and rural appearance of the south shore, the side used by fishermen, has been preserved. Further along that shore stand a group of school buildings, followed by the "Promenade des Impressionnistes" on the water's edge, built in collaboration with the architect Jean-Louis Fortin. On the opposite shore there is a succession of raised spaces where the walker finds himself nearly always above the level of the environment, with fine vistas toward the distance, and plantings that mask the unsightly constructions or industrial buildings on the banks of the Seine facing the island.

051

Sketches by Jacques Simon for the Ile Saint-Denis Park.

Views of the north and south banks of the park.

When the Tuileries Palace was
burned down by the Commune in
1871, then demolished in 1882,
it was replaced by flower beds
in the taste of the times. The new
plantings attempt to recover the
same 19th-century spirit.

Pascal Cribier

With a degree in plastic arts from the Ecole des Beaux-Arts in 1976 and another in architecture two years later, nothing seemed to destin Pascal Cribier for a career in landscape architecture. It was the fruit of a chance encounter. Back in his native Normandy, Cribier went to work for horticulturists and tree nurseries. There he acquired his technical skills as well as a taste for landscape. And there too he met the individuals responsible for the shift in his professional life: the city-planner Patrick Ecoutin, with whom he made a four-year study on the architecture and landscape of Pays de Caux, and the clients who gave him his first commissions. Gradually he became known through his private gardens. But his real claim to fame was attained with a project that was to put him in the media limelight—in 1990, he won the competition, together with Benech and Roubaud, for the rehabilitation of the Tuileries Gardens in Paris. Since then, Cribier's practice has grown. With architects Philippe Starck and Arsène Henry, he completed the garden of the Ecole des Arts Décoratifs. Associated with Lionel Guibert, he won the competition for the park at the Fort of Aubervilliers and worked on the restoration of the park and creation of the garden at Woolton House, Newbury, England. Cribier, always pragmatic, takes a humanist approach to his projects. With a gardener's sensitivity, he knows the value of bare spaces. He seeks the birth of emotion—fragile, unique and ephemeral—that lets the visitor stop for a moment, look around and comprehend.

053

The restoration of the Tuileries Gardens have restored the traces of Le Nôtre's design, which prefigured the famous westward perspective.

In a picturesque medieval setting,
around the Viollet-le-Duc-style tower,
a minimalist garden underscores
the contrast between the centuries.

Pascal Cribier

This is a private garden in the Oise Department. It belongs to a professional art auctioneer as well as a collector, two pursuits which are not incompatible. The setting is astonishing: a manor house where, it is said, Joan of Arc once slept, a Gothic chapel restored by Gustave Eiffel and a castle keep reconstructed in the spirit of Viollet-le-Duc. The owner wanted Pascal Cribier to landscape the grounds in order to open them to the public as a venue for exhibitions of contemporary art. Perched over the Vallée de l'Automne, the design of the garden is flat and offers small-scale perspectives. The proportions of the pool and the subtle differences in height of the lawns were calculated with precision. The play of colors, with blue dominating, is created by masses of flax and iris. The collision between medieval imagery and the geometric abstraction of Cribier's work produces the dramatic look that was sought by both client and landscape architect.

055

Pascal Cribier

Pascal Cribier

Dominated by the mass
of the stone walls, the
garden seems suspended
over the pool in a deliberate
and subtle theatrical way.
The ground, which seems flat
at first glance, is actually
sculpted by slight differences
of level and height of grass,
accentuated by the regular
spacing of flax and iris,
in shades ranging from
deepest to palest blue.

Pascal Cribier

At the foot of the walls,
the iris tufts are aligned
in a rigorous geometric order.

Pascal Cribier

Pascal Cribier

Pascal Cribier

The farm of La Coquetterie is situated in Normandy, in the Pays de Caux, with its rolling hills and hedge-crossed farmland. It is made up of one-third cultivated fields, one-third pasture land and one-third forest. The first commission Cribier received from the owner, Madame de Bagneux, was to redesign the immediate surroundings of the house and create a kitchen garden that would not demand too much upkeep—on a working farm, all hands are needed for the farm work. To this rather banal request, Pascal Cribier brought an answer based on geometric minimalism. He laid out 36 squares, alternating herbs, vegetables and flowers. The gravel paths, wide enough for a tractor to pass, are also used for parking cars. This checkerboard links the house to the stables. On another part of the property, at the foot of rolling hills, a ravine typical of the region is overgrown with woods. In 1751 three clearings had been made and bordered with spruce. Struck by disease, most of these trees had to be removed in 1995. Madame de Bagneux then asked Cribier to work on this wooded area. In a first "green room" in front of the only row of spruces that had survived, Cribier planted three slopes with juniper bushes, in diagonal lines for a rhythmic effect. The clearing is closed by three rows of birch. The second is bordered by beech and nut trees with, at its heart, a cage of prunus, golden in autumn and snowy white in spring. For the third clearing, Cribier intends to use three varieties of beech, in three contrasting colors.

The potager of La Coquetterie:
a series of square beds, each planted with a single
variety of vegetables, flowers or aromatic herbs
and surrounded by gravel paths, extends from
the house to the stable.

It is bordered by a line of wooden posts topped
by flower pots.

Along the path, a bench with Art Nouveau
arabesques by Claude Lalanne.

Pascal Cribier

A reconstituted "green room."
The little clearing called the
"prunus cage" is ringed by beech
and nut trees.

Opposite page:
Three hornbeams with their tripod
stakes line the passage between
the potager and the lawn, which
extends to the edge of the woods.

In front of the half-timbered house
typical of the region stands
an army of boxwood balls.

Pascal Cribier

If Alain Richert were ever
to create a collection
—an unlikely prospect given
his nomadic inclinations—
it would consist of irises.
The pond adjoining his house
in the Dombes region
is surrounded by white irises.

Alain Richert

Alain Richert is a curious spirit, a dilettante in the original sense of the word. He studied medicine in Lyon and ran a gallery of contemporary art. He has done painting, photography and calligraphy, and exhibited his works in Paris: *"There is nothing orthodox in my itinerary. I went from painting to carpets, and the interest in carpets led me to gardens."* Which, after all, is not too surprising when we remember that Persian princes had transposed onto carpets the image of the garden–"paradise" in Persian.

Richert set out as an autodidact to learn about botany, ornithology, horticulture and the history of gardens:

"I learned botany in a cemetery. It was a cemetery of English aviators that I crossed every day as I went to get milk for my son. I would pick plants and try to identify them when I got back home. When I had exhausted all the plants in the cemetery, I went on to those of the slopes and graveled paths. I would concentrate on one type at a time to study its diversity. The classification of Linnaeus reads like something organized by a lawyer. That of Michel Adanson, botaniste royal *at the Trianon garden, and his essential work,* Familles de plantes, *were truly encyclopedic projects."*

Richert did his first garden, for himself, on an abandoned industrial site. At the workshops he leads at the Ecole nationale supérieure du paysage de Versailles on the theme "Art of gardens, art in gardens," he develops the relationships between the art of gardening, the history of art and an awareness of our times–its culture and its modernity.

What answer can we bring? And to what question? How to invent an art of living in a troubled society?

"A garden, by definition, responds to a question turned to tomorrow, not to the old preoccupation of 'it was better yesterday.'" For Alain Richert, the role of the artist is not to give an answer, but rather to ask a question. As for resolving technical problems, that is not what creates a garden. *"If the technique is visible, the garden is a failure. Technique concerns no one but the technician. And for this expert botanist, if the garden sometimes speaks of plants, the plants, for their part, do not necessarily speak of the garden."*

The terrace connecting the yard
to the house combines vegetal
and mineral in one rigorous
composition: Burgundy stone,
thyme and alchemilla framed
by lines of treated oak. Mown
meadow and flowered prairie
alternate up to the broad ditch
placed at the edge of the property
to avoid fencing off the garden.

Alain Richert

According to Alain Richert, the quality of a garden depends in large part to the attentive care of owners and gardeners.

This is the case for one of his projects, a garden in the Dombes region designed for a dentist, owner of an aquarium and lover of tropical fish, whose rigor and assiduity in the maintenance of the garden are a tribute to its creator: *"I consulted other landscape gardeners and looked through many gardening magazines. No one was able to establish, as Alain Richert did, such a dialogue between this house, the terrain and the landscape. Here the garden constitutes a sort of frame, interdependent with the house."*

The thermal-treated oak beams between which are embedded the Burgundy stone pavers alternate with the plants, thyme or alchemilla, and stretch toward the horizon.

The pool of water was sunk into the clayey soil with no ground sheet underneath, and it fills with water depending on the seasons. Around the pool, an emblematic flower, the iris in two white varieties which bloom in succession: Iris germanica and sibirica.

Alain Richert does not make a general plan. He jots down some notes in the form of sketches, then compiles his list of plants. The rigor and sophistication we feel in the progression from lawn to prairie only seem all the more natural.

067

Alain Richert

La Guyonnière castle:
view from the drawbridge with
the garden reflected in the water.
Green rooms succeed one another
in the medieval manner from
one level to the next.

Alain Richert

Alain Richert

Perhaps it was the influence of his first commission, a monastery garden for the chartreuse de la Verne, in the Var, but Alain Richert enjoys flirting with the Middle Ages. It was a period of great curiosity about plants, both as food and as a source of medicine, and he sees working with medieval sites as an exciting challenge.

Richert allows himself great freedom of approach when creating—or re-creating—a medieval garden. *"It's the eternal question: is historical truth to be found in exact reconstitution, or in preserving a certain intention and attitude through ever-evolving techniques and materials? In a word, can tradition survive by simply being frozen?"*

The creation of a garden in la Guyonnière castle in Poitou-Charentes was posed in those terms. The garden is on an island which you reach by a drawbridge after crossing the courtyard of a 14th-century construction. It is encircled by a raised promenade planted with oak and chestnut trees. Two bowers of old roses and grape vines lead to nine thematic "rooms" with such evocative names as *Le Clos des Petits Fruits* or *Le Jardin des Papillons*. These theme gardens follow in succession, one after the other, until they reach the open countryside.

Opposite page:

Behind the little medieval manor, a passage under an arbor leads to a meadow where concerts are held in summer. At the other end of the island, a simple gate allows the gaze to wander over the countryside.

An attic window, the only vantage point on the garden from the house.

071

Alain Richert

A platform of wooden pavers
set into the carefully mowed
lawns announces the garden of
perennials. The paths are marked
by gates and boundary lines.
Roses and grapevines intertwine
on the arched bowers.

Alain Richert

Alain Richert

Erik Borja

On a rugged terrain in the Drôme Department countryside, where peach orchards and vineyards dominate, Erik Borja has made a natural sculpted space with a Mediterranean character strongly tinged by zen philosophy.

"I was restoring a house in which I intended to set up my studio, and to go with it, I designed a simple, pleasant little garden. I had nothing particular in mind, no idea of making it a work of art, but it changed my life. When I began spending more time in the garden than I did in the studio, I realized the change was irreversible."

In 1979 Erik Borja, architect, sculptor, draughtsman, artist and photographer, decided to get away from the agitation of Paris and its exhibitions and moved into an old winegrower's house in the Drôme. A trip to Japan in 1976 had already been a revelation for him. He was very taken with a philosophy that treats gardening as an examination of oneself as well as an approach to art. He found the extreme economy in the Japanese use of water, space and plants, all the more fascinating as he remembered with wonderment the profusion of flowers in the gardens and patios of his childhood in Algiers.

Poetry of place, observation of nature, work on the mineral element— stones or mountains, control of water and vegetation, are so many elements that fueled his conversion. Noting: *"You can't leave a garden as you leave a painting,"* he proceeded to become increasingly attached to this new form of expression.

The choice of the Drôme Department was no accident. Borja's father has a peach orchard there, and the garden is encircled by terraces that go all the way down to his father's peach trees. These levels of sculpted vegetation and elaborately-shaped boxwood gradually lead the visitor toward the ponds. There, on the scale of a natural landscape in miniature, the islands and rocks take on Japanese overtones while still belonging to a very personal vision of the site. The philosophy of zen is in no way inimical to these terraced slopes of the Mediterranean. The approach of Borja the gardener is projected in time: he has already made the sketches for the clipping of a cypress to be done 50 years from now...

The former house of a winegrower overlooks a dense
garden punctuated by basalt columns taken from
the chimneys of volcanos in the Haute-Loire Department.
Their colors vary with the light and humidity. Beyond
the rolling waves of *Lonicera nitida*, a *Juniperus* trimmed
in a cloud shape in the Japanese tradition.

Erik Borja

Erik Borja

At the back of the garden, a pond surrounded by Mediterranean species that Borja carefully disciplines. The combination of mineral, vegetal and aquatic opened an unexplored field of action for the gardener cum sculptor.

A paving of ancient cobblestones from the town of Romans laid irregularly around a composition of terra cotta fragments and roof tiles that were dredged from the river.

Opposite page:

Behind the sculpted bench of *Lonicera nitida,* at the edge of the garden, stand a pine, some crab apples and the peach orchard.

Erik Borja

Erik Borja

Erik Borja

The house towers over a steep terrain that descends to the sea. To the rocks already there, Borja added blocks of stone cut from the mountain, and for the vegetation, he combined deep green with pale acid green.

In a skillful framing by the architect, the rocks efface the limits of the garden and bring the sea into the composition.

The mastery of landscape and fine knowledge of Mediterranean vegetation that he acquired in working on his own garden were invaluable for Borja in creating this garden in Corsica, which occupies 3,500 square meters of a 1.5-hectare estate. Affronting the surrounding maquis, he transported rocks and stones, structured the vegetation and added plants found in the mountains as well as shrubs chosen for their interesting shapes and their resistance to wind and salt. He sculpted the terrain and temporized with the elements. As always, he took great pains with framing, bringing the panorama into the garden and paid special attention to the different pathways, from garden to beach or from garden to the surrounding countryside.

The careful placing of rocks helps to anchor the garden on its slope and in its overall terrain. Whether prairies or underbrush, the vegetation is controlled. Trees have been removed to open views on the sea.

Borja's assimilation of Japanese techniques and his familiarity with Mediterranean soil have come together to give birth to a garden that is subtle and sober, with an elegant sensuality.

Erik Borja

082

Erik Borja

A trail leads down to the shore
through trees and shrubs of the
maquis. Under green oaks, Borja
kept a cactus because he liked
its shape, and trimmed into ball
shapes the myrtles, mastics
and Corsican rosemary.

Rocks mark the passage
from the prairie to underbrush.

Erik Borja

Right:
In a hollow in the garden,
a pool surrounded by rocks
in which are anchored little ferns
brought in from Antibes.

Species borrowed from
the neighboring maquis were
chosen for their resistance
to the wind and sea spray.

Erik Borja

Erik Borja

La Vallée, in the Creuse
Department, is first of all
a piece of fallow land where
Gilles Clément chose to plant
his own garden and implement
his idea of the "Garden in
Movement." With the help of
a friend, he then built the house
for the garden, in the spirit of
the architect/carpenters
of the United States.

Gilles Clément

In 1990, when Gilles Clément published his very personal work, *The Garden in Movement*, the little manifesto came like a bolt from the blue. It not only created a stir, it also set the tone for his future research, and for his courses at the Ecole nationale supérieure du paysage de Versailles.

An inveterate traveler, photographer, writer, and entomologist, Gilles Clément has scoured the landscapes of the planet and synthesized along the way a certain number of ideas that had been in the air since the 1970s.

To illustrate his ideas, this agricultural economist and botanist stopped one day in a valley in the Creuse to make his garden, on a piece of unused land that would serve as the laboratory of his reflection. The land in question was not being worked but could be—a state of affairs that is essentially dynamic. When a piece of land is left to itself, it creates the necessary conditions for the earth to receive dozens of different species. It is a place with no taboos, holding all the *"ordinary richness of nature."*

The gardener makes no claim to manage the invasion, but accepts it and orients it to his advantage, to turn it into a garden. Its design is in his hands, movement is his tool, grass his matter, life his field of knowledge.

"To make a place for oneself in nature without having to combat it—that is the ideal of the garden I was aiming at. Of course, there's still a way to go."
Clément's work questions the entire notion of order that has marked both the agricultural landscape and the history of gardening.

This idea of a garden in movement would be integrated into his design for the André-Citroën Park in Paris in the early 1990's. Here, a vast public would come to appreciate both the free open spaces and the theme gardens, where the discovery of plants is made under the sign of color.

But Clément is constantly broadening his field of reflection. He returns from each voyage of discovery with the profound feeling that the exchange and intermingling of cultures are gradually wiping out the notion of distance. Thus, for the Rayol Littoral Conservatory, he composed a medley of Mediterranean type landscapes, and borrowed from the vegetation of Chile, South Africa, China, Australia and New Zealand.

"The emergence of ecology has revolutionized the relation of man to nature. Once he was master of the world, now he is part of it, forced to respect the forms of life on Earth. His future depends on it."
Today Gilles Clément is working on the notion of a "planetary garden." On this idea, he has written a fictional treatment, *Thomas et le Voyageur*, which has been the theme of his exhibition at La Villette for the year 2000.

Gilles Clément left in place the existing trees and shrubs, like this gray willow *Salix cinerea*, which is trimmed each year. It offers a formal counterpoint to the islands of shrubs and grasses preserved in this natural garden.

088

On the slopes of La Vallée, the abandoned land has slowly been transformed into a garden and new plantings subtly introduced. In the foreground, the red ochre sebum "Autumn Joy" a silver *Santolina neapolitana* and a tuft of *Stipa gigantea*.

Gilles Clément

089

A tree trunk uprooted during
a violent storm and five others
cut down after the storm bear
a strong resemblance to a bridge
and a set of stepping stones.
Is one a ford for animals
and the other for human beings?

A spontaneous invasion of daisies
and digitalis has found a home
amid the herbs and vegetables,
in the squares of the old
kitchen garden.

Gilles Clément

Gilles Clément

Opposite page:

On the prairie, amid the original feed crops, a blanket of flowers with foxglove clearly standing out, and beneath, tall stalks of Aaron's rod, evening primrose and echium.

A close-up of a very simple rose, *Rosa Moyesii* "geranium" which blooms in June and in autumn produces very decorative orange fruit.

A small maple, *Acer griseum*, whose copper red bark flakes off every autumn.

Stipa tenuifolia growing out of the bedrock.

Gilles Clément

Along the promenade that dominates the serial gardens, separated by channels, pools and water stairways, small greenhouses present various plant scenes.

Opposite page:
At one end of the park, separated by 80 jets of water, stand the two large greenhouses of wood, metal and glass designed by architect Patrick Berger. One shelters tropical species, the other is used for temporary exhibitions.

Gilles Clément

Situated in a new neighborhood of the 15th Arrondissement, the André-Citroën Park is built on an axis perpendicular to the Seine, as are a number of older Paris parks—the Jardin des Plantes, the Esplanade des Invalides and the Champs-de-Mars. More surprising is the X-shaped outline of the park within the limits of the yet-to-be-completed surrounding buildings.

Following a competition organized by the City of Paris in 1985, two co-winners shared the 14 hectares reserved for this green space on the site of the former Citroën auto plant on the Quai de Javel: Gilles Clément and the architect Patrick Berger, on one hand, and the landscaper Alain Provost with the architects Jean-Paul Viguier and Jean-François Jodry on the other. A diagonal line across the great lawn, the *tapis vert,* separates the gardens of the two designers. This green space created from scratch is quite different from other Paris parks. The paradox is that it is a strong structure, but one that leaves visitors a great liberty. Around the lawn, a space for games and recreation, the designers have provided a multitude of propositions—in form, a profusion of theme gardens. Two peripheral gardens, symmetrically placed at the

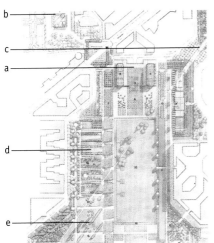

upper edge of the park, the White Garden and the Black Garden, represent the extremes in this idea of colors. The idea is then developed in blue, green, orange, red, silver and gold in the serial gardens, treated on the scale of a private garden.

At the lower end of the park, toward the river, is the "Garden in Movement," installed on 1.5 hectares, punctuated with hothouses, canals, water staircases. The idea of a garden managed like fallow land is now left to the skills of the gardeners.

"It is entirely in their hands; the type of maintenance required by the garden in movement takes them out of the role of mere caretakers to which they are usually relegated."

For visitors, being part of the implementation of an experiment is a stimulating experience, and they enter the spirit of the place, trying to recapture some of the lost liberty of nature.

093

Set among residential and office buildings, the André-Citroën Park unfolds a broad green carpet, crossed by a diagonal to separate the gardens of its two designers, Alain Provost and Gilles Clément.
a) Large greenhouses
b) White Garden
c) Black Garden
d) Serial Gardens
e) Garden in Movement

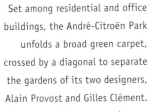

Gilles Clément

Opposite page:

The Green Garden, devoted to the sense of hearing, is planted with *Miscanthus sinensis* grasses, which rustle in the wind. It has striking green flowers, such as hellebores, heracleum, alchemilla and the amazing green rose, *Rosa viridiflora,* half moss-like, half pompon-like flowers.

Below:

More astonishing yet, the red-thorned *Rosa sericea*, in the Garden in Movement.

Right:

The Orange Garden, representing the sense of touch, plays on different ground textures. A design symbolizing a stream marks the smoothness of the concrete path, which crosses an expanse of pebbles, rough and irregular.

At the foot of the water stairs, on the other side of the walk that runs along the serial gardens, water lilies communicate with the grand canal surrounding the lawn.

Gilles Clément

The principle of the Garden in Movement is based on plant dynamics. The art consists of choosing the proportion of plants that you allow to go to seed (and which will propagate freely), in contrast to those you choose to cut. The cutting creates trails and clearings, pathways changing with the passing years.

Giant thistles, *Onopordum arabicum*, grow in complete freedom.

Another view of the Green Garden. In the foreground, leaves of *Peltiphyllum peltatum*.

Opposite page:
From the Blue Garden comes the scent of sage, wisteria and mint, a garden of smell with a clever medley of colorful plants that lets the blue stand out and creates a fluid transition toward the Garden in Movement.

Gilles Clément

Continuation of the schist staircase of Hispano-Moorish inspiration bordered by cypresses was created by Gilles Clément.

Southern ferns (*Dicksonia antarctica*) and *Cyathea cooperi* scattered in the prairie of South African freesia.

Gilles Clément

This superb domain of 20 hectares, situated on the Mediterranean coast between Le Lavandou and Saint-Tropez, was acquired by the Shoreline Conservatory, whose purpose is to protect seashores and their ecological abundance. Adopted in 1989, the project consists of safeguarding first of all some 15 hectares of shoreline *maquis,* plus a 5-hectare garden already planted with completely acclimated exotic species—eucalyptus, palm trees, acacias, etc.

As project manager, Gilles Clément set out to create new landscape settings. Through his travels and his personal research, he compared the types of vegetation associated with the Mediterranean climate with those of other regions that enjoy similar climatic conditions. He made an inventory of magnificent trees that had resisted extreme frost, and recreated for plants of other continents *"landscape entities, pieces of landscape"*: a prairie of New Zealand carex, a mallee of shrub eucalyptus and Australian "black boys", a moor of Chilean puyas, a valley of tree ferns and South African fynbos.

The Domain of Le Rayol also functions as an experimental territory, where a number of plants present have an atavistic ability to live with fire. Some species have developed astonishing faculties of adaptation and can quickly reconquer the burned terrain. The reflection of Gilles Clément hinges on the relation between science and landscape: *"The possibility of fire as a tool of landscape management must be must be taken into account. It is a biological reality about which every human being on earth should be aware."*

099

Jardin Chilien Jardin Californien
Jardin Sud-africain Jardin Australien
Jardin Chinois Jardin Neo-Zélandais
Jardin marin Jardin d'Amérique centrale aride
Jardin d'Amérique centrale sub-tropicale

La ferme
Pergola
Le bastidon
Entrée
"L'hôtel de la Mer"
Anse du figuier

Le verger
Le puits
Le potager

Itinéraire 30 mn
Itinéraire 1h. 30

Pointe du figuier
"La Villa"

Gilles Clément

Upstream, the New Zealand
garden shows off its "tea trees",
Cordyline australis
and *Olearia scillonensis*.

Below
A New Zealand landscape
resembling the grassy plains
in the center of South Island.

Gilles Clément

Gilles Clément

Dragon trees and echium
from the Canary Islands.

In the Central America Garden,
yucca and agave plants surround
a group of candlestick cacti.

Gilles Clément

Kathryn Gustafson

An expatriate in Paris from the northwest coast of the United States (which was and still is the cradle of contemporary landscape architecture), a textile designer before attending the Ecole nationale supérieure du paysage de Versailles–Kathryn Gustafson offers a subtle example of a landscape practitioner who reconciles strongly-contrasting attitudes in France and the United States. From the French school she doubtless took her solid technical and horticultural training, as well as a tendency to consider the landscape as a cement for social considerations. From her American origins she inherited three fundamental characteristics of her approach: a pragmatism that never forgets that any response found must be correct for the program, the site and the client; an inclination to link poetry and psychology, filtered through childhood memories and personal feelings and, lastly, a manner of treating the landscape as a sculpture on the scale of territory in the tradition of *"land art."*

Gustafson's method is in line with this logic. It proceeds first of all from a meticulous analysis of the site and the program, and extends into the history of the place in order to determine any particularities. After this first phase is completed, Gustafson searches her own feelings for a relation she can establish with the future user or spectator. This introspection is accompanied by a work on form through small-scale clay models that the artist fashions by hand and which are later produced in plaster. Her miniature sculptures show a deliberate plasticity, which will serve to fashion the landscape, just as she once used textile, with ample folds and ripples that will be transcribed in the land.

On the terrain itself, she exhibits a tranquil audacity. Perhaps her complicity with the great English or American engineers, Peter Rice, Martin Francis and Ian Ritchie, with whom she collaborated for the greenhouse of the Science Museum of La Villette, has given Gustafson the assurance that technically all is possible; the idea of moving thousands of cubic meters of earth is a challenge that doesn't phase her at all. This assurance, added to her sensitivity and fine-tuned sense of poetry, has inspired the confidence of public clients and large firms like Shell, Esso or L'Oréal. She uses a supple geometry, visions based on different scales, and carefully-selected materials: the stone that marks the limits of the vegetation, the metal that often punctuates the site with a distinctive sign, water in quiet pools, canals or playful fountains.

Her designs in Marseille, Terrasson-La-Villedieu or in the Paris area have won Kathryn Gustafson an international reputation. Today she divides her practice between London, Amsterdam, Paris and a little island near Seattle, Vashon Island in Puget Sound.

At Terrasson-La-Villedieu a long promenade dotted with water jets borders a small straight channel.

Kathryn Gustafson

With the worthy aim of developing tourism in their lovely region, the town fathers of Terrasson-La-Villedieu, in the heart of a beautiful rural area of Périgord, launched in 1992 a limited-entry competition for a project to be entitled "The Five Continents." The name implied the use of references to the most famous gardens in the history of the world. A 6-hectare site overlooking the old town, a panorama over the valley of the Vézère, old oaks, maples and acacias, fields of high grass and wild flowers and a few cisterns of the old drainage system formed the framework of the project.

Kathryn Gustafson and the team of Paysage Land carefully avoided the two obvious traps: that of post-modernist pastiche and an overly literal citing of natural representations that are no longer in use. They deliberately limited their response to a contemporary interpretation of figures and motifs that have marked the history of gardens. The park invites its users on a journey more sensual than didactic: perspective, layout, elements (water, wind, and plant life) find their place in a plan that brings out the natural qualities of the site. The visitor is invited on a "landscape tour" (just as a former generation used to exalt the architectural tour), punctuated by poetically charged events.

As soon as you enter the site, the tone is set by a series of pylons topped with metal weather vanes: you are going to see the wind, and also hear it by means of hanging bells. The stations of the suggested itinerary are those found in the original park, barely modified to create pathways.

107

Another manner of using water
in a playful spirit: here
it cascades down a staircase cut
into the steep slope
of the terrain.

Kathryn Gustafson

Kathryn Gustafson

Opposite page:

Close-up on the rose garden and its metal structure. In the distance one can make out the roofs of the old town of Terrasson-La-Villedieu.

The path, curved or straight, the presence of water, stairs at various points along the slopes, all make up a precise itinerary with a feeling of informal freedom.

A perspective and an embankment dotted with waterfalls, a pergola rose garden, a golden strip marking the path to the "Gardens of the elements" where one can see the hybridization process of azaleas, Montpellier maples, ferns and mosses, the greenhouse designed by Ian Ritchie, set between gabions (freestone walls held in place by wire mesh), the amphitheater with its metal benches, the cruciform water garden in the style of Persian or Mongol gardens, a fragment of topiary and a "sacred wood" with its clearing of wildflowers—all these constitute a varied and animated sequence, on a background of views from above over the town and the valley.

A rest area in the form of an amphitheater offers a view on the old town.

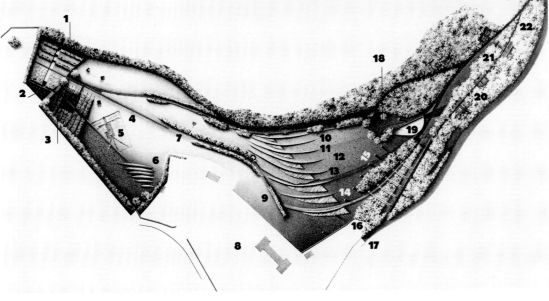

Master Plan

1. Terraces
2. Water jets
3. Rose garden
4. Canal
5. Ephemeral trace
6. Lower pools
7. Fountain path
8. Retirement home
9. Topiary
10. Forest path
11. Amphitheater path
12. Perspective
13. Fountain path
14. Sacred wood path
15. Wind axis
16. Entrance
17. Amphitheater
18. Greenhouse
19. Sacred wood
20. Ticket office
21. Golden thread
22. Gardens of the Elements

Kathryn Gustafson

The relation with the building's architecture is clearly stated; linearity of the building versus the supple relief of the lawns.

A clear geometric layout orders the rectilinear paths and lines of the fencing along the canals.

Kathryn Gustafson

The gardener's task here was to integrate a new building on a plot of land along the Seine riverfront. The project aims to create a new urban entity that respects the character and scale of the existing buildings.

The lines of the garden correspond to the shadow cast by the building and the curves of the plan repose on the junction points of the shadows at the moments of solstice and equinox.

The garden's dominant color is the silver green of its hedges and weeping willows. The central garden uses the existing vegetation of the riverbanks. The hedges, sometimes parallel and sometimes perpendicular to the river, make the transition between the existing and the newly built.

The main entrance is marked by a long pool that forms a cascade over a bank of steps alongside a ramp. The pool is fed by a series of canals that stagger the change of level between the building and river.

Along the bank a broad platform overlooks the river and forms a space of repose, which Gustafson has provided with two sleek curved benches, ironically named the "earth-cutter" and the "water-gazer."

The access to the building is by broad steps parallel to flowing water.

The direct relation to the river is materialized by the mineral terrace and a bench called the "water-gazer".

111

Kathryn Gustafson

Desvigne & Dalnoky

Desvigne and Dalnoky appeared on the French scene just at the time when landscape architecture, though still largely linked to public commissions, was losing a bit of its subservience to social affairs and its role as a mere enhancer, something to make up for the failures of a botched city planning. Their training at Versailles, reinforced by their work with the agencies of Corajoud and Chemetoff, had stressed rigorous analysis of the site, an analysis that tended to focus too much on signs of the past and to put esthetics in the forefront of the project. In their eyes, the French milieu had yielded to a certain formalism, even bordering on the academic, expressed by a tendency to "over-design" and use of the diagonal or even the serpentine curve of Mannerism. A stay at the Villa Medicis, in a Rome steeped inescapably in memory, allowed them to see its limits. Back in France and back to practice, Desvigne and Dalnoky were convinced of the need to exercise restraint. They also felt it was time for a landscaping project that would be totally modern, in which the analysis of the site with the help of the latest techniques, notably satellite photos, would be only the backdrop. This drive to move forward was probably accelerated by their familiarization with the Anglo-Saxon milieu and landscape.

Rue de Meaux, Paris

An inner courtyard, a sloping terrain carpeted with rambling honeysuckle, rectilinear walkways and white birches whose trunks accord nicely with the rhythm of the façades.

A courtyard in the 19th Arrondissement of Paris, a project on a modest scale commissioned by the architect Renzo Piano, whose only expressed wish was: "For God's sake, no diagonals!" Desvigne and Dalnoky drew rectilinear alleys as logical extensions of the lines of the building facade. They used the slope of the terrain in two ways: a longitudinal path of a constant level ends in a staircase of a few steps, while its parallel turns into a slight ramp over the sloping land planted with a thick carpet of rambling honeysuckle. The slim trunks of randomly planted white birches play with the verticals in the structure of the building facades. The paths are covered with the same terra cotta as the panels on the facades and the concrete casings that hold the lighting equipment are the same width as the uprights, showing an understated intention to remain in tune with the building.

Desvigne & Dalnoky

Creating a link between two parks on the Colline de Fourvière gave Desvigne and Dalnoky an occasion for a slight intervention. In a delicate context, it clearly illustrated their wish not to commit anything irreversible. The crest of the hill bore the traces of an old tram line, unused in recent years except for transporting coffins to the hillside cemetery. This nearly invisible line enabled them to open negotiations with the religious authorities that owned the domains over which the viaduct once ran. In this location, Desvigne and Dalnoky installed a long walkway between the two public spaces. The walkway, designed by the architect Manuelle Gautrand, became a promenade that offered views down into the convent gardens below. The supports of the viaduct were preserved as well as the machinery of a funicular, and the wooden planks that form the footbridge can easily be dismantled. Should the need arise, the site remains open to any future project.

The Colline de Fourvière bears the traces of an old viaduct. The architect Manuelle Gautrand has used its piers to install a metal structure, which supports a footbridge punctuated with belvederes. Walkers can enjoy the serenity of the gardens below, which belong to different religious communities established on the hill since time immemorial.

116

The promenade offers spectacular
views over the river and the city,
and unusual angles on the
Fourvière Basilica and Lyon's
Paufique Tower.

Desvigne & Dalnoky

A park not so much urban as bucolic, developed on both banks of the Théols River, on land once occupied by abandoned orchards and vegetable gardens. The landscape architects chose to accentuate a large square planted in oblique lines, to recall the plots formerly on the site.

We tend to ignore the slow mutation of the rural landscape by the processes that fashion and modify the territory, except when a sudden problem with major infrastructures—a railroad line, dam or motorway—reminds us. In the rural region of Berry, in the very center of France, gradual depopulation has, almost imperceptibly, created empty spaces. In Issoudun, a picturesque village crossed by the Théols River, a tributary of the Cher, Desvigne and Dalnoky have accomplished a modest project: to make an urban park (the word is perhaps excessive) out of what was once a river bank covered with orchards and vegetable gardens. The character and scale of the nearby town did not lend themselves to any heroic gesture. Taking a "leave well enough alone" approach, the landscape architects designed a plan with an understated geometry. They followed the lost lines of the former garden plots, planted carefully-chosen species in square, dense parterres, and built wooden decks, barely touching the ground, to form walkways that end by slightly jutting out over the river. The park recalls the forgotten scent of evening promenades, and a little air of the provinces, where it feels good to be...

119

120

The pathways through the park
are marked by simple wooden
decks whose ends jut out over
the river.

François Brun and Michel Péna came to landscape architecture by very different paths. Brun had studied biology and organic chemistry. Péna, a graduate of the Bordeaux school of architecture, had discovered landscaping during a walking tour of France. They met at the Ecole nationale supérieure du paysage de Versailles and began to work together, notably on a project for the André-Citroën Park competition—a project that did not go unnoticed. Invited to enter the competition for the park over the Montparnasse railroad tracks, they won the project, which would later be known as the "Jardin atlantique." This work, beset with the greatest difficulties, would keep them busy until 1994, and earned them a well-deserved recognition.

Afterward, each pursued an independent career. Brun worked on rehabilitation projects of deteriorated natural sites, like the riverbanks at Montesson and Melun, but also did landscaping for public housing projects, and headed the landscaping plan for the urban community of Cherbourg. As for Péna, he has worked intensely, together with his wife Christine, on a great number of projects, many of them still in progress: city squares in Lyon, the town center of Chatellerault, a public park on the Seine riverfront in Croissy, etc.

The Atlantic Garden, Paris

The Atlantic Garden, enclosed on four sides by modern buildings some 50 meters high, is built on a vast concrete slab that covers train tracks and parking facilities and demands stairwell openings and emergency exits. An unlikely place for a public park, but its creators have managed to overcome all the hazards.

The operation Maine-Montparnasse, as it was known at the time, was realized between 1958 and 1973. The old railroad station had been demolished and a new one built further to the south, leaving space for a complex of modern buildings, including a 58-story high-rise. Around the new station, and parallel to the tracks for some 200 meters, are three low-rise structures, 50 meters in height. The developers, the SNCF (French State Railway Company) and the city of Paris, had promised the tenants of the buildings and others living or working in the area a park to be built on a concrete platform of 4.5 hectares to be built over the tracks. But once the buildings were completed, they quickly forgot their promise. Complaints were answered with technical and financial arguments. When work began on a new set of offices which would straddle the tracks and close off the perspective, the arguments (specious to be begin with) could no longer hold. The SNCF was modifying the station to receive the new high-speed train, the TGV. It was the moment to kill two birds with one stone.

The competition, opened in 1987, called for the realization of a 3.5-hectare garden on a simple low-cost platform over a structure of posts and beams well-suited to bearing an equally-distributed weight. But this plan did not reckon with the ambitions of the SNCF, which wanted (and rightly so) to give its prestigious new TGV train a space with an architecture worthy of it. Thus the landscapers saw themselves saddled with a platform that had 36 good-sized openings and a structure more capable of bearing weight in the shaded areas than in the sun. A parking facility underneath determined a grid whose lines had to be 16 meters apart. As an additional constraint, for security purposes, they had to have a peripheral road and a median avenue to allow the passage of fire engines. The winning design by the young landscaping team of François and Christine Brun and Michel Péna was probably chosen because of their refusal to accept fatality and the liberties they took with the program. A large lawn in the center, equipped with a sculptural structure in the shape of an arch (under which the fire engines can pass), a sequence of theme gardens 16 meters wide, "waves" of soil to counter the unequal load, walkways in the form of footbridges over the vegetation, were among the clever means they used to circumvent the technical difficulties. The planting of tall trees was impossible, so all the species chosen, both trees and shrubs, had to accommodate themselves (stretching out their roots horizontally, if necessary) to a total volume of soil varying from 30 centimeters to 1.80 meters.

Drawing inspiration from the Montparnasse station, which serves Brittany and the Atlantic coast, Brun and Péna developed an oceanic theme that is not without a certain picturesque charm. In the cold implacable geometry of the surrounding buildings, they probably needed the riot of shapes, colors and materials—pink granite from Brittany, blue marble from Brazil, sand and rocks of various sorts—to compose a parable on an ocean theme that can distract the visitor from the very close presence of the city and the train station. The Atlantic Garden—the name chosen by the team—provides a variety of open air activities for young and old alike, and offers a welcome change of scene in the bustle of the city.

Brun & Péna

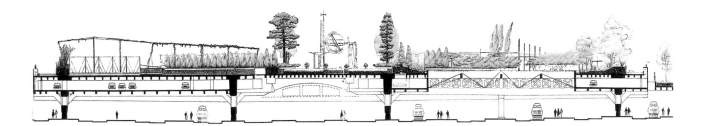

Longitudinal cross-section. Below the garden, the railroad station, but also the parking space, aeration facilities and emergency exits, each a further constraint added to the site which should also be endowed with a supporting platform.

Opposite page and left: Very mineral at the outset, the garden has slowly been conquered by trees, shrubs and perennials. The massive waves of grass evoke the freedom of wide open spaces, creating a genuine change of scene in the heart of Paris.

Brun & Péna

A raised walkway passes over
the grasses, then penetrates
the underbrush beneath weeping
willows. The choice of ground-
cover under the trees has made
a difference in giving these walking
paths a feeling of privacy.

Brun & Péna

Another constraint:
an access road for fire engines
cuts the garden in two by
a passageway 6 meters wide.
To break up this expanse,
they installed the "Isles of
the Hesperides," both a weather
station and a children's water park.

Brun & Péna

Bruel & Delmar

Anne-Sylvie Bruel and Christophe Delmar belong to the new generation of landscape architects trained at Versailles by the renowned figures whose reflection formed the new foundations of the discipline in France. It is to their teachings, multiple and complementary, that students owe the diversity of their skills: Chemetoff for an awareness of scale and painstaking attention to detail; Corajoud for the discipline of the drawing board and the "judo strategy," where the project draws strength from its own difficulty; and Clément for a profound understanding of the plant world and the dynamics of time.

Bruel and Delmar begin with a rigorous analysis of all the constituents of a landscape, an approach that permits them to take on the most varied genres—urban installations, gardens or projects in rural areas.

"When you take up a project, you must consider its relation to the place where it is located, the specificity of its history, culture, geography, a specific land division or architectural style, in any case, to a topography that forms the basis of the site."

Biville

When Bruel and Delmar set about replanting a site devastated by the working of a quarry, they were able to restore a "natural" landscape that makes their work all but invisible.

Anne-Sylvie Bruel and Christophe Delmar were freshly graduated from the Ecole nationale supérieure du payage de Versailles when they were chosen to rehabilitate a former quarry at Biville, a project that consisted in nothing less than bringing back to life a zone that had been devastated by years of stone extraction.

They knew what they were in for: *"We had already worked on catastrophe sites—a dam on the Loire with 20 meters of marl deposits, a valley crossed by the embankment fills of the TGV line. It is as if they had called in a landscape architect as a last resort, as a kind of therapist of lost causes."*

The community of Biville, with 400 inhabitants, is in the north of the Cotentin Peninsula, at the tip of La Hague, a stone's throw from the nuclear waste processing plants. When the working gravel quarry situated on town land shut down, the decision was made to create a rural park in its place. The open gash in the earth's surface was spectacular. At one point in the road, the cutting face looms up before you, gaunt and majestic, stretching 450 meters long and 40 meters deep to well below the level of the valley floor. The project covers 7 hectares. The site contains various

130

Fed from surrounding springs,
a pond had formed on the valley
floor. The consolidation of the
shores and introduction of aquatic
plants aided the reproduction
of fish. Two staircases descend
to the water, one of broom
and one of *gabions*.

Gabions, a technique that
consists of building a dry stone
wall under a wire mesh support.
Here, stone fragments from the
quarry protect the main staircase
from erosion, while permitting
water to run off freely.

Bruel & Delmar

Bruel & Delmar

types of vegetation: prairies on the plateau, woods on the valley slopes and moorland on the steep hillsides. The terrain is scattered with ravines and landslides, and encumbered by the sterile residue of the quarried gravel.

To answer questions of an ecological nature, the team called upon an expert, Prof. Montégu, an ecologist specialized in adventive plants and the recolonization of land covered with rock debris.

The two aspects of the program were replanting the site on the one hand and creating a recreation area on the other.

The rhythm they adopted made it possible to work with the landscape in its evolution over time. The blighted terrain was prepared in such a way as to stabilize the soil and permit the return of durable vegetation. The first steps of the reclamation consisted of building restanques, retaining walls, on the steep slopes to avoid the formation of gullies, collecting the run-off water and the fine silt, bringing in vegetal species that would compensate for the deficiencies of the soil, and lastly, recolonizing the soil through the natural sowing of gorse and broom, which bring in organic material and also serve at windbreaks, all essential elements in the reconstitution of soil and implantation of new species.

The option chosen was to keep the cutting face, whose operation is part of the history of the town and which gives the site its force and originality. The surrounding springs have filled the valley floor and a natural pool has formed at the bottom of the quarry. Two stairways have been built leading down from the cutting face. The shores of the pond have been given a particular treatment, based on the fact that the most popular leisure activity here is fishing. A risberme, a platform installed below water level, serves to maintain the bank and create a safety zone. The planting of aquatic plants has aided the reproduction of fish. With family outings every Sunday and a popular fireworks display on Bastille Day, the park has now been adopted by all the inhabitants.

Anne-Sylvie Bruel and Christophe Delmar are well aware that the integration of the park into the landscape is a slow process. *"You have to wait five years, maybe ten, for the project to come to life, and 20 years for the pines, flattened by the wind, to be replaced by oaks. You wait for the dynamic of the plant world to do its work and forget that landscape architects took a hand here long ago."*

133

From the jetty, a favorite spot
with fishermen, we can see
the visible part of the 40 meters
of rock face, which so vividly
recalls the former quarry;
the other half is submerged
beneath the waters.

Bruel & Delmar

The Pont du Gard, the handsome
Roman aqueduct spanning the
Gard River, is the region's major
tourist attraction as well as an
ecological site whose protection
requires specific planning.

Laure Quoniam

"The art of constructing landscapes and gardens combines in a single profession my taste for painting, my interest in nature and a desire to build in a way that is different from what can be expressed by architecture."

An an architect herself, graduated from the Ecole des beaux-arts in 1979, Laure Quoniam found her vocation in the United States. After a master's at Harvard in 1985, she had an internship with Dan Kiley, one of the most famous of American landscape architects. She learned the impact of a discipline long recognized and organized across the Atlantic, in which the first quality of a landscape is its power, a criterion considered more important than its "beauty." Back in Paris, having acquired the self-confidence needed to run a business, she opened her own agency in 1991.

"The New World taught me professionalism, but it also taught me to appreciate tradition, history and local background, though always from a certain distance. I became fascinated with garden history. The same year I started my agency, I obtained a position with the Culture Ministry as advisor for the restoration of private gardens. That gave me the opportunity to visit gardens and make assessments throughout France for a whole year."

The 1992 Pont du Gard project, calling for the protection of a historic and ecological site, raised a complex and very basic question: how to reconcile the dream of retrieving a "natural nature" with the reality that the site had to be reorganized to accommodate 2 million visitors a year. The same year, Quoniam staged for the first Festival of Gardens in Chaumont-sur-Loire an evocative "Garden of the Senses," based on the theme of Zola's novel, *La Faute de l'Abbé Mouret.* In 1994 she designed an emblematic vegetable garden for the headquarters of the Food Processing Center in Saint-Lo, Normandy, and also redesigned the interior garden and the surroundings of the RATP (public transport authority) Headquarters in Paris.

For the Pont du Gard as for the Jardin d'Acclimatation, Quoniam made use of the magic of virtual images to construct her projects in three dimensions, like a tableau vivant.

"I like to build space using the infinite richness of the mineral and vegetable world. I like to compose its lines, shapes and colors, modulate its light and shade..."

Roman civilization has left its mark on Provence, the "provincia romana" of the Roman Empire. Of all the monuments that show the genius of Roman engineering, this gigantic aqueduct is perhaps the apotheosis. The Pont du Gard rises up at the last turning of the Nîmes highway and the sudden discovery is all the more spectacular as the site is seen from below. The relief of the hills and the present layout of the site do not allow for distant views which would enable a gradual approach to the monument in its surroundings. The impact of the monument spanning the high banks of the Gard river also comes from the coherence of the surrounding scenery.

For Laure Quoniam, the point of the landscaping project is to maintain intact the harmony that has always existed between the bridge and its setting, to keep alive that dream aspect that the Pont du Gard has always inspired.

The remains of the Aqueduct of Nîmes, the backbone of the project, represent the major interest of the visit. The fact that visitors have an overall view of the landscape from the bridge allows them to understand the course of the canalization, which follows the topography of the site over the 50 kilometers, between Uzès and Nimes, that separates the source from the Roman Baths. A 360° view makes it possible to read the course and appreciate the technical prowess. Cut into the folds of the earth, through hollows of the rock and the wooded parcels of the garrigue, the line of the long canal is sometimes clearly visible, sometimes barely discernible.

This project for developing the site must hinge on several levels: archeology, around the remains of the canalization, the museography which tells its own history, and the touristic possibilities, which range from hiking or riding trails to the discovery of a natural park.

The landscape architect's work aims to improve the appearance of the approaches to the viaduct as well as to enhance the surrounding plateau.

Laure Quoniam

The project is organized round two public entrances, each with its own parking area, on the Balouzière plateau in the north and on the plain in the south. The bridge is the pivot of visitor circulation, the aim being to counterbalance the visits on both sides of the river. Each entrance has reception facilities informing visitors of the different routes to follow and activities offered.

The protection of the historic and ecological Pont du Gard site belongs to no classic planning category. For Laure Quoniam the debate is based on the nature of the restoration that will show the bridge to best advantage. *"This debate has been going on for ten years now. It is difficult because the concern about restoring major heritage sites is a recent one. One by one, the public authorities and the different participants in the project had more experience with protection of buildings than of a living site, which is by definition evolving and fragile. Time is a crucial factor and must be considered as one of the basic components of the project."*

VUE AERIENNE DE L'ETAT EXISTANT

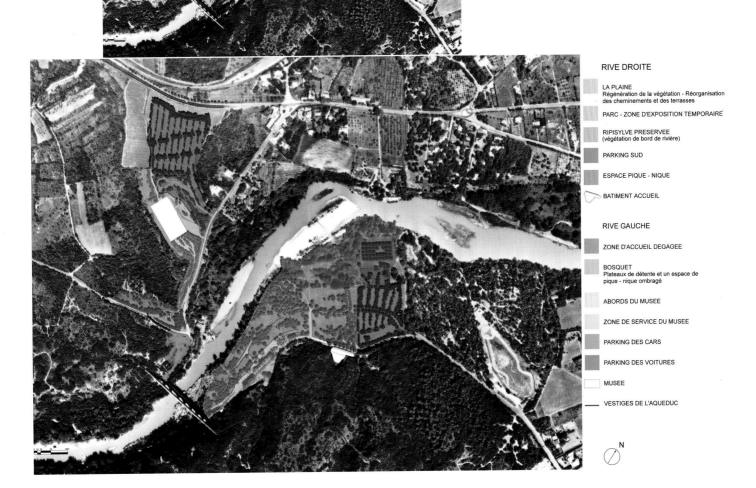

RIVE DROITE

LA PLAINE
Régénération de la végétation - Réorganisation des cheminements et des terrasses

PARC - ZONE D'EXPOSITION TEMPORAIRE

RIPISYLVE PRESERVEE
(végétation de bord de rivière)

PARKING SUD

ESPACE PIQUE - NIQUE

BATIMENT ACCUEIL

RIVE GAUCHE

ZONE D'ACCUEIL DEGAGEE

BOSQUET
Plateaux de détente et un espace de pique - nique ombragé

ABORDS DU MUSEE

ZONE DE SERVICE DU MUSEE

PARKING DES CARS

PARKING DES VOITURES

MUSEE

VESTIGES DE L'AQUEDUC

N

137

Laure Quoniam

Botany magnified by computer technology: in the projected creation of Laure Quoniam, broad-leafed plants like *Gunnera* and *Fatsia* and giant flowers like these oversized sunflowers, cabbages and grasses create a dreamlike landscape on a scale that is totally unreal, with no familiar reference points.

Laure Quoniam

Laure Quoniam has invented a verdant space for children to play in that is full of creative freshness, while respecting the vocation of the initial garden.

The garden, originally created by the Société d'Acclimatation, opened in 1860, to offer city dwellers in search of exotica a recreational space filled with flora imported from "distant climes" and fauna "acclimated" to our hemisphere. Started as a zoo, it later became a children's park. But today, when everyone has access, directly or indirectly, to all the landscapes in the world, the wonders of an unknown nature have lost much of their force.

Quoniam's design for this space makes no reference to any real landscape genre, nor to one of the clichés of landscape—jungle, desert or equatorial forest. Rather, it springs from a common fund of imagination linked to childhood.

She found in literature a source of wonder that could be constructed from natural elements and thus transposed to a real space—a play on improbable scales, as in *Alice in Wonderland* or *Gulliver's Travels*, or its more recent cinema equivalent, the film *Microcosmos*.

The theme she chose is in tune with this principle of discrepancy of scale: the world of insects. The plastic richness of the arthropod species leaves a large place to interpretation of games adapted to different age groups.

The planting of vegetation and the drawing of the plan alternate opaque areas with open space, under the cover of existing tall trees. The pathways organized between plant masses and game "rooms" offer surprise effects.

A series of "rooms" set within a maze.

Each "room" develops a theme of its own: the one called Flight is devoted to swings and jumping games; Metamorphosis is for sliding games; the Anthill offers obstacle courses and treasure hunts; Cobwebs and Beehives is for climbing; the Observation room for interactive activities and games based on optics; and the room of Mists has wading pools and games of hide-and-seek.

139

Opposite page:

The Room of Mists, where children play hide-and-seek. Giant spider webs woven between plantings.

Laure Quoniam

Below:
A cast-iron sculpture, 21 meters long and positioned on granite supports, meanders through a beech grove alongside a lake. This work by Australian sculptor David Jones, entitled *Green Place for Red Ants*, (1988), refers to the three natural orders— animal, vegetable and mineral.

Vassivière

The Contemporary Art Center of Vassivière in the Limousin Region is a singular institution on the French artistic scene.

The site is astonishing in itself: a lake of 1000 hectares created by a hydro-electric dam put into service in 1951, a shore whose vegetation adapted itself to the lines traced by the engineers and to the rise of the waters, then to a tourism activity based on water sports. Now an island stands in the center of the lake; it measures 70 hectares and rises to a height of 700 meters.

In the early 1980's, the regional and interdepartmental authority of Vassivière acquired the island and invited artists to come and work in the region. Living with local families, in a spartan and secluded environment, these pioneers worked with wood and granite, combined with water and other natural elements.

Beginning in 1983, a footbridge was built to the mainland and the works started being shown on the island. From the outset the idea was to use the spot as a place of creation. With the arrival of Dominique Marchès, in charge of a project for a Contemporary Art Center, a new era opened, favored by cultural decentralization.

The design of the building by architect Aldo Rossi brings a poetic response to the imposing construction of the dam. Built of granite and brick on a slight rise in the very middle of the park, the edifice and its lighthouse-like tower are gracefully installed in the natural site. They house temporary exhibitions, multi-functional spaces, a library and bookshop, a cafeteria and an artist's studio.

The location of the Vassivière Center, far from any art scene, assures it a large measure of freedom. Naturally devoted to sculpture and intended in time to constitute an open-air museum, the center has gradually evolved, thanks to various artists invited to create *in situ*, in a different and unexpected direction. The works in the park, which proceed from natural resources, tend to modify the perception of the landscape and the island is slowly being transformed.

Two Sheepfolds (1992),
an installation by Scotsman Andy
Goldworthy. A wall of stones in
the shape of a question mark,
built with the remains of a stone
wall that once ringed a field.
The immersion of the stones
evokes the villages drowned by
the filling of the dam.

Descending Vessel (1989)
by Welshman David Nash for this
tree that threatened to fall and
thanks to the vision of the artist
seems destined to become a skiff.

Vassivière

Erreurs-exact (1994) by Anne-Marie Jugnet.
Two neon signs lost amid the foliage: a play on contrasts that brings out the contradiction
between nature and technology. A work in the moralistic spirit of Barbara Kruger and Jenny Holzer.

Vassivière

erreurs

Vassivière

A living work of art made of plaited
willows by British artists Judy and
Dave Drew. The stalks, planted and
braided, take root in several weeks,
then sprout leaves and metamorphose
into a labyrinth that will thicken
and solidify with the passing years.

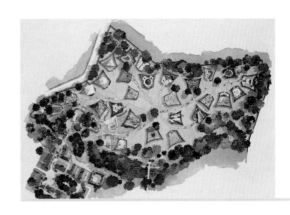

Garden Festival, Chaumont-sur-Loire

"Thirty gardens for one summer"—this was the idea launched in 1992 by Jean-Paul Pigeat under the auspices of the International Conservatory of Parks, Gardens and Landscape. Since then the International Garden Festival has presented every year in the park of Goualoup, Chaumont-sur-Loire, 30 garden events created by landscape architects from France and abroad on irregular plots of land, convex or concave, each about 250 square meters. Along with the official selection are invited a number of well-known figures who are apt to bring a fresh approach to the art of gardening. They include artists, architects, decorators, choreographers or photographers... Known from the outset for showmanship and stirring emotions, Chaumont can surprise or amuse as well as astonish or irritate. The Festival completely overturns the received idea that a garden is always planned, designed and realized over a period of time, and not something that springs up in one short year, as is the case in Chaumont.

With humorous or provocative themes like Imagination in Crisis, Poetically Correct, Gardens of Curiosity, Water water everywhere, or Ricochets—the festival is a veritable kaleidoscope of inventive images. No one who has seen them has ever forgotten the Leak in the Caravan by Macha Makéieff, Willows in the Mist by Judy and David Drew, Waterfall of Bucket on a Bed of Peppermint by Michel Desvigne and Christine Dalnoky, the Bamboo Tunnel by the filmmaker Hiroshi Teshigahara, the Great White Meadow of 3000 white cosmos by Mark Rudkin, the Scale of Corn Growth by Bob Wilson, the Double Boiler Vegetable Garden by the Agence européenne du paysage or the Growing Walls by the botanist Patrick Blanc erected several years in a row. Growing plant species without soil is a technical feat: thanks to calculated heights and orientations, walls can create microclimates, which in turn permit the development of original plants. Chaumont does not exist merely to arouse curiosity. It is also a laboratory of botanical research. To assure the rapid growth of the 30 gardens selected each year, Chaumont needed the services of a virtuoso botanist. They found one in the person of Eric Ossart, who sets up and follows through on the projects, conceived by gardeners from every corner of the planet. Ossart made nasturtiums and other climbing plants soar upwards on 195 fiberglass fishing rods by Swedish landscaper Monika Gora, tuned the sunflowers and solar panels of Peter Walker, and given life to the spiral path leading to the summit of a tumulus by George Hargreaves... Outside of the "showing season," which lasts from June 15 to Oct. 15, the Conservatory plays a year-round role in the renewal of many aspects of the landscape arts: adult education, seminars and serving as a research and documentation center.

Every year since 1992, the Chaumont Festival (ground plan above) presents 30 gardens, ephemeral in principle, on 250 square-meter plots laid out by landscape architect Jacques Wirtz.

Opposite page:

New England Garden by Lynden B. Miller: a mix of plants—asters, eupatorium, rudbeckia, soligado— and styles borrowed from both Europe and the United States.

Chaumont-sur-Loire

But for all their serious pursuits, the people at Chaumont periodically show a sense of humor. In the summer of 1998, for example, they ran a series of "Special Days" of a rather unusual kind: there were "Horror Days," where children were invited to get lost in the woods, discover monstrous plants, eat repulsive stewed fruit and learn the dullest of lessons; "Nothing Days," which were not advertised, and about which no one even knew how many there were, or what was going to happen. In any case, for visitors who did show up, there were no activities and no rewards... except perhaps the reward of spending a quiet day with gardeners and philosophers.

The composition of parsley and flowers around a bed of cabbages: rows of red feather and French marigolds alternate with *Cosmos sulphureus*, dahlia and calendula... At Chaumont, the farmyard serves as an experimental field of annuals for botanist Eric Ossart.

Soft Greenhouse
by Edouard François and Duncan
Lewis (1996) shelters exotic
plants, water lilies and papyrus.
Its structure is of bamboo stalks,
its skin of supple transparent
plastic attached by strings
to bamboo of a rustic variety
(*phyllostachys*).

Chaumont-sur-Loire

Growing Walls by Patrick Blanc and Michel
Mangematin (1994-1997):
plants and shrubs cling to a felt carpet
nourished with mineral salts by automatic
closed circuit watering, from pools that
collect water at the foot of the wall.
Different inclinations and exposures
favor microclimates suitable for varied
vegetation. Here a fig tree perched
on top of the wall has reached a spread
of 5 meters in 3 years.

The Mediterranean Garden
by Eric Ossart:
maquis plants contained
by *gabions*—stone walls held
together by wire mesh, very
common in southern France.

Chaumont-sur-Loire

Gently falls the dew...
A strange-looking water
device by J. Sordoillet,
A. Sotto, V. Martinez, 1998.
Structures of stretched netting
that resemble morning glories
collect the mist of the night.

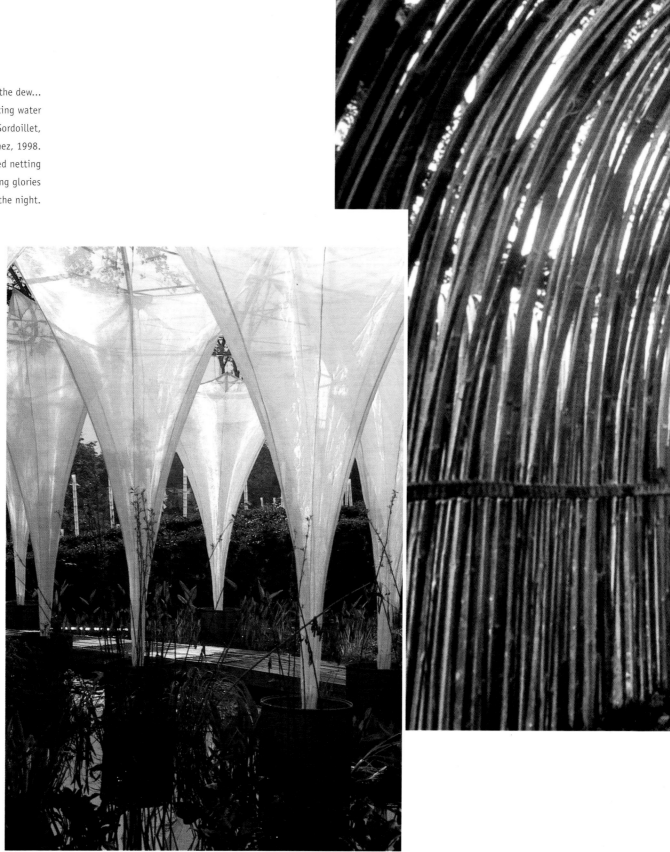

The Bamboo Tunnel (1992),
its floor strewn with pine needles, a pathway of initiation created
by filmmaker Hiroshi Teshigahara, director of *Woman in the Dunes*.

Chaumont-sur-Loire

Reflected on a dark still sheet of
water, the photo of a nude and
the shadows of the garden,
a composition by Keiichi Tahara
(1998).

An archipelago of polished black
stones, a study in *satori*, on a sea
of carefully raked white gravel.
A symbol of the crisis in Japan
and hope for a better world,
evoked by Shodo Suzuki
(1993-1998).

154

Aquatic garden by Michèle Elsair and Jan-Pierre Delettre (1996-1997). Surrounded by giant leaves, a dark pool is divided into five lanes to create five different aquatic variations: concentric circles caused by a falling drop of water, waves created by the movements of a bin, shimmering waves made by a stream of air, a wake traced by the movement of a metal fin set in motion by the visitor, and last, bubbles that rise from the bottom of the pool and burst at the surface among water lettuce.

Erik BORJA

Born in Algiers, 1941.
Graduated from Beaux-Arts, Algiers, in architecture
and sculpture. 1963: works in Paris on fractioning and
recomposition of images through mirror structures.
1973: begins his garden in the Drôme, where he sculpts
his first plants. 1979: settles there permanently.
Major works
1986: designs gardens for individuals or communities.
For the city of Romans, Drôme department: 1987: René Char
garden. 1992: gardens for Musée International
de la Chaussure, and Couvent de La Visitation

Anne-Sylvie BRUEL and Christophe DELMAR

Born in 1961 and 1962 respectively.
1986: Bruel: DPLG diploma in landscaping from ENSP,
Versailles, after studies in biology.
1989: Delmar: DPLG diploma in landscaping from ENSP,
Versailles, after studying horticulture at Ecole du Breuil
and early studies in architecture.
1989: founded their agency, Atelier de paysages, in Paris.
Since 1997: Bruel and Delmar lead a 3rd-year workshop
on landscape and habitat at ENSP.
Major works
1990: park at quarry of Biville, Manche , with E. Ossart
and L. Collin (landscape architects) and J. Montegut (botanist). 1995: beach of Pampelonne, Ramatuelle. 1998:
new gardens of Salagon, Haute-Provence ; rebuilding dam
in Nancy and dock rehabilitation, Meurthe-and-Moselle. 1998:
terraced gardens, Château de Charance, Gap, Hautes-Alpes.

François BRUN

Born in 1957.
1983: graduated from ENSP. Studies in biology and bioche-
mistry. 1983-1990: association with Michel Péna.
1990: opened his own agency.
Landscaping consultant for the Ministry of Equipment in Vendée.
Major works
1994: Jardin atlantique. 1992-: Park of Trevarez.
In progress: public plazas in Saint-Etienne and Lyon ;
rehabilitation of public housing (3 000 units) in Paris suburbs; redesign of the banks of the Seine in Montesson,
of Saint-Etienne island in Melun and the banks of the Vire
River in St-Lô (in progress).

Michel PÉNA

Born at Bouscat, Gironde, 1955.
Architecture studies in Bordeaux. 1983: graduated from
ENSP. Independent work as landscape architect.
Until 1985, worked occasionally with Chemetoff's agency,
Bureau des paysages.
Major works
1994: Jardin atlantique, Paris. 1992: Mercedes plant in
Lorraine ; 5 kilometers of planting along ring road of
Bordeaux. In progress: two plazas in Lyon ; planting for the
Nantes tram line ; creation of a recycling center in
Bordeaux; creation of a public park on the banks of the
Seine at Croissy-sur-Seine.

Alexandre CHEMETOFF

Born in Paris, 1950.
1970-1973: studies in Landscape and Garden Arts section at
ENSH. 1977: DPLG diploma as landscape architect.
1974: founds group Carré Vert with Jacques Coulon,
Alain Marguerit and Claire Corajoud. 1983: founds his agency, the Bureau des Paysages. 1987-1989: teaches at ENSH.
Since 1990: teaches at School of Architecture, University
of Paris-Tolbiac.

Major works
1983-1986: gardens of French Embassy, New-Delhi, India.
1985-1992: Bièvre Valley rehabilitation project,
in Val de Marne department. 1985: Bamboo Garden, park
of La Villette, Paris. 1988-1989: design for surroundings
of Finance Ministry, Paris-Bercy. 1991-1993 Place de la Bourse,
Lyon. 1992-1995: Le Havre Beach. 1991: rehabilitation project, banks of Vilaine River; public and private space
for urban development zones of Le Mail and La Malibais,
Rennes. 1993-: public and sports park Géo-André,
La Courneuve. 1997-: design of Port Henri-IV for the Paris
port authority. 1998: design of entrances to Stade de France,
Saint-Denis.

Gilles CLÉMENT

Born at Argenton-sur-Creuse, 1943.
1967: engineering degree from ENSH. 1969: DPLG diploma
from ENSP.
1976: opens his agency in Paris. Lecturer at École
d'Architecture, Versailles and workshops at ENSP.
Major works
1977-: La Vallée, Creuse, experimentation site of Jardin
en mouvement. 1987: grounds of Château de Bénouville,
Provence. 1986-1988: gardens of Valloires Abbey, Somme.
1986-1992: park André-Citroën, Paris (project shared
with Alain Provost). 1992-1994: Terre vivante, Domaine
de Raud, Isère. 991-1997: garden at the Arche de la Défense
(with Guillaume Geoffroy-Dechaume.) 1988-1997: Domaine
du Rayol, Provence. 1992-1997: park Henri-Matisse, Lille
(with Empreinte). 1997: design for metro line, Lausanne-
Ouchy, Switzerland.

Michel and Claire CORAJOUD

Michel: born in Annecy, 1937.
Student at Arts Décoratifs, Paris. 1964-1966: works with
Jacques Simon.
1966-1975: member of AUA (Atelier d'urbanisme and d'architecture).
1971-1974: leads workshop in landscaping section, ENSH,
Versailles. Since 1977: teaches at ENSP.
Claire: born in 1945.
Studied until 1968 at Beaux Arts, Paris.
E.N.S.P. 1969 - 1972 (D.P.L.G.). C.N.E.R.P. (National
research center for landscape) 1973. Member of the group
Carré Vert - 1974.
1979: both of them found their agency in Paris.
1992: Grand Prix du Paysage.
1993: Prix du Courrier du Maire for urban project "Ville
de Montreuil".
Major works
1974: park of Coudrays, Maurepas-Élancourt, and park
of Grenoble-Villeneuve (with AUA). Since 1981: park
of Sausset. 1994: redesign of city boulevard urbain at Cité
Internationale, Paris. 1996: and of Cité Internationale,
Lyon; extension of La Tête d'or park (with Renzo Piano).
1997: design for roof of A1 autoroute, Saint-Denis; redesign
project for Avenue d'Italie, Paris.

Jacques COULON

Born in Angers, 1947.
Student at the Ecole des Arts décoratifs and des Beaux-Arts
(workshop of Etienne Martin). 1970-1972: studies at ENSH,
landscape section.
1974: DPLG diploma in landscape architecture.
1974: member of group Carré vert with Alexandre Chemetoff,
Alain Marguerit and Claire Corajoud.
Independent landscape architect based in Paris.
Since 1977: teaches at ENSP de Versailles.

Major works
1997: public garden and pedestrian access paths,
Porte d'Aubervilliers, Paris. 1996: design of Place du Forum,
university campus,Orléans-la-Source, Orléans. 1990:
rehabilitation of Cité des Martinets, Montataire (Oise) ;
redesign of seaside promenade, Saint-Valéry-en-Caux.
1995-: promenade along Marne River, Maisons-Alfort and
Marne-La-Vallée. 1997-: renovation of Agora and surrounding
quarters, Athens (Greece).

Pascal CRIBIER

Born in Louviers, 1953.
1976: diploma of plastic arts, Ecole des beaux-arts.
1978: DPLG in architecture. Independent landscape architect, works jointly on some projects.
1992-1995: teaches in the architecture section Arts décoratifs.
Since 1992: works with CEAAP of gardens and landscapes,
École d'Architecture, Versailles.
1993: leads a workshop at ENSP.
Major works
1982-1998: restructured area around La Coquetterie, Limésy
(Normandy) and forest clearings ; garden of Donjon de Vez
(Oise) ; patios of Opéra-Bastille (Paris) with
F. Roubaud ; garden for International Conference Center,
quai Branly, Paris (with Alain Provost) ; restructuring
of Tuileries gardens, Paris (with L. Benech and F. Roubaud) ;
urban park of Bussy Saint-Georges, Seine-et-Marne.
In progress: garden at Woolton House, Newbury, England
(with Lionel Guibert) ; rehabilitation of park at Méry-sur-Oise
and creation de gardens for Vivendi/Générale des Eaux
(with J.M. Wilmotte and Lionel Guibert).

Michel DESVIGNE and Christine DALNOKY

Born respectively in 1958 and 1956.
1979-1983: Michel Desvigne studies botany and geology.
1983: Enters ENSP. 1974-1978: Christine Dalnoky studies at
Beaux-Arts, Paris. 1978: Enters ENSP (diploma in 1982).
Until 1986, both work with Michel Corajoud and Alexandre
Chemetoff. 1986-1988: together, they win first place for the
Prix de Rome in landscaping ; two years of study at Villa
Médicis. 1988: creation of their agency and projects with
various architects (Renzo Piano, Norman Foster, Valode and
Pistre, Paul Andreu, Jean-Marie Duthilleuil, Jean Nouvel).
Since 1985: teach at ENSP.
Major works:
1990: Garden, Rue de Meaux, Paris, (with Renzo Piano).
1991: Place des Célestins, Lyon (with F. Neveux, B. Rouyer
and P. Lévy, Lyon). 1992: design of gardens, parking areas,
prairies and forests for Thomson plant at Guyancourt (Renzo
Piano architect). 1996: access Roissy-Charles de Gaulle
Airport. 1994: urban park on banks of Théols River,
Issoudun, (Indre). In progress: viaduct at Avignon, Vaucluse;
TGV station Valence, Avignon, Marseille; Millenium Park,
Greenwich (with Richard Rogers).

Kathryn GUSTAFSON

Born in Seattle, USA, 1951.
1971: studies fashion design at The Fashion Institute
of Technology, New York, 1971. 1979: graduated from ENSP.
1992: Équerre d'argent award. 1993: Architecture medal
from Académie d'architecture française for all of her work.
Major works
1986: design of the large greenhouse (La Grande Serre)
at Cité de la Villette, 1991: landscape design for Shell
Headquarters, Rueil-Malmaison (with Melissa Brown) ;
design for surrounding area of Esso Headquarters, Rueil-
Malmaison ; Place des Droits de l'Homme in Evry (Essonne).
1992: landscape design around Oréal factory, Aulnay-
la-Barbière (with Isabelle Lafuma). 1995: design of highway
interchange, Autoroutes A7/A 55, Marseille (with Philippe
Marchand and Pierre Solbes) ; new design for high tension

pylons for EDF (with I. Ritchie, architect) ; park at
Terrasson la Villedieu "Continent de l'imaginaire"
(with Anton James and Philippe Marchand). 1997: "Son
éphémère et jardins de vent" in Lausanne, Switzerland (with
composer François Paris).
In progress: Crystal Palace Park, London ; landscape design
of Seattle stadium and exhibition center (with Landscape
Architects Anderson & Ray).

Laure QUONIAM

Born in 1952.
1979: DPLG degree in architecture from Ecole des Beaux-
Arts, Paris (1979). 1985: master's of Landcape Architecture
from Harvard. 1991: opens her agency in Paris. 1991: advisor for restoration of historic private gardens for the heritage
preservation authority. 1998: begins teaching at Ecole
supérieure d'architecture des jardins.
Major works
Many private gardens. 1992: redesigns garden of Hôtel
du Vieux-Logis in Dordogne. 1984: rehabilitation of banks
of the Marne for the city of Saint-Maur (with D. Collin and
A. Schuch). 1993-: historic and ecological rehalilitation of
site of Pont du Gard (with P. Viguier, architect).
1994-1995: creation of interior garden remodeling of
exterior space for RATP headquarters, Paris (with P. Sirvin,
architect). In progress: landscape design of the Port de
la Rapée.

Alain RICHERT

Born in Fez, Morocco, 1947.
1964-1971: studies medicine in Lyon. Studies gardening
independently. 1976-: studies botany, ornithology, horticulture and history of gardening. 1977: assistant to Edouard
Avdeew in Paris. 1979: advisor in botany for the shop
Despalles, Paris ; directs a documentary film on the park of
Varengeville. 1981: advisor for a series of 12 TV programs
on plants and gardens for Antenne 2. 1984: heads a landscaping workshop at École d'architecture de Versailles.
1988-: heads workshop "Art des jardins, art dans les jardins" at
ENSP. 1994-: consultant for gardens at Thoiry (plant/animal relations). Since 1996-: consultant for the Jardin de labyrinthes
at Reignac, Indre et Loire.
Major works
Many private gardens, including Les Dombes and
La Guyonnière. 1978: creation of an arboretum and medieval
garden, Ballon, Sarthe. 1980: cloister garden of the
Chartreuse de Villeneuve-lès-Avignon, Vaucluse.
1985: gardens of Château d'Ô, Orne. 1987: "Labyrinthe aux
Oiseaux", Gardens of the Five Senses, Yvoire, Savoie.
1997: heraldry garden, Mondelazac, Aveyron.

Jacques SIMON

Born in Dijon, 1929.
École des Beaux-arts, Montreal. Graduated from ENSP.
1968: creation of the magazine *Espaces verts*, after first
journalistic experience with the magazine *Urbanisme*.
1990: First Grand Prix du paysage.
Teaches at ENSP, Versailles, and at universities of Toronto,
Pomona in Los Angeles and Harvard.
Major works
1970: park Saint-John-Perse, Reims. Juillet 1989:
ephemeral creations, pages of geography, poetic and
political messages, such as Marianne (Orly Airport).
June-July 1990: European Flag (Turny, Yonne).
1992: Hands Off My Earth! (Turny). 1993: Wild Kiss (Turny).
1995: garden-city of Plessis-Robinson (Hauts-de-Seine).
1996: motorway rest area at Villeroy.

General Bibliography

Benoist-Méchin Jacques, *L'homme et ses jardins, ou les métamorphoses du Paradis terrestre*, Paris, Albin Michel, 1975. ● Dubost Françoise, *Vert patrimoine: la constitution d'un nouveau domaine patrimonial*, Paris, Éditions de la Maison des sciences de l'homme, 1994 . Hobhouse Penelope, *Plants in Garden History*, London, Pavilion Books, Ltd. 1992. Imbert Dorothée, *The Modernist Garden in France,* London, Yale University Press, 1993. Le Dantec Jean-Pierre and Denise, *Reading the French Garden,* Cambridge 1990. ● Mosser Monique and Teyssot Georges (Dir. by), *The History of Garden Design*, London, Thames and Hudson, 1991. ● Pigeat Jean-Paul, *Parcs et Jardins contemporains*, Paris, la Maison rustique, 1990. ● Racine Michel, *Jardins en France: le guide des 750 jardins remarquables*, Arles, Actes Sud, 1997. ● *Paysage méditerranéen*, Milan, Electa, 1992. ● Auricoste Isabelle, "Le rouge et le vert" (with A. Vulbeau) in *l'Ivre de Pierres* n°4, 1983, "L'enclos enchanté" in Mythes et Arts, 1983, "Les formes du paradis" in *Paysage et Aménagement*, 1986, "De l'espace urbain" in *Parc Ville Villette* Champvallon, 1987.

Symposium Proceedings
Alain Roger (sous la dir.), *Théorie du paysage en France, 1974-1994*, Seyssel, ChampVallon, 1995.
Claude Eveno et Gilles Clément avec la coll. de Sylvie Groueff, *Le Jardin planétaire*, Éditions de l'aube, 1997

Erik Borja
Erik Borja ; photographies de Paul Maurer, *Rencontre dans un jardin*, Romans, musée de Romans

Anne-Sylvie Bruel et Christophe Delmar
Pages Paysages: territoires, "reconversion d'un site stérile" n°4, 1992/93 . *Pages Paysages:* contacts, "Pièges à sable", n°6, 1996/97 . *Techniques et Architectures*, "Aménagement d'une carrière, Biville", n°403, août-sept. 1992

François Brun et Michel Péna
Techniques et architecture: le paysage en question ; août-septembre 1992, n°403. *Pages paysages:* contacts, "Jardin Atlantique", n°6, 96/97 . *Landscape Architecture*, "Gift from the sea."

Chaumont
Arnaud Maurières, Eric Ossart, Laure Boucrot, *Jardins nomades, tapis de fleurs: 20 modèles de fleurissement saisonnier*, Aix-en-Provence, Édisud, 1997 . Arnaud Maurières. (sous la dir.), *Guide des jardins botaniques de France*, Pandora, 1991 . Jean-Paul Pigeat, *Parcs et jardins contemporains*/Paris, la Maison rustique, 1990.

Alexandre Chemetoff
Alexandre Chemetoff ; photos Elizabeth Lennard, *Le Jardin de bambous au parc de La Villette*, Paris, Hazan, 1997 . *L'Architecture d'aujourd'hui*, Alexandre Chemetoff, n°303 février 1996 . *Topos European Landscape Magazine*, "Der Strand von Le Havre", Munich, n°13 . Alexandre Chemetoff, Conférences Paris d'architectes 1994 au pavillon de l'Arsenal, Ed. du Pavillon de l'Arsenal, 1996

Gilles Clément
Gilles Clément, *Le Jardin en mouvement: de la vallée au parc André-Citroën*, Sens et Tonka, 1994 . Gilles Clément, *Une école buissonière,* Paris, Hazan, 1997 . Gilles Clément, *Les Libres Jardins de Gilles Clément*, Paris, éditions du Chêne, coll. les grands jardiniers, 1997 . Claude Eveno et Gilles Clément avec la coll. de Sylvie Groueff, *Le Jardin planétaire*, Éditions de l'aube, 1997

Michel Corajoud
Techniques et architecture, "La part commune", septembre 1992 . *L'Architecture d'Aujourd'hui*: Paysages, "Parc du Sausset, projet Lauréat", n° 218, décembre 1981 d'Architectures, "Apologie du complexe", n° 29, octobre 1992 . Alain Roger (dir.), *La Théorie du paysage en France, 1974-1994*, Seyssel: Champ Vallon, coll. Pays/Paysages, 1995 . Paysages.- in *L'Architecture d'Aujourd'hui*, décembre 1981, n°218 . *L'Architecture d'Aujourd'hui*: "Paysage", n° 262, avril 1989

Jacques Coulon
L'Architecture d'Aujourd'hui: Paysages, "Concours d'idées pour l'aménagement du parc départemental du Sausset", n° 218, décembre 1981 . *Pages paysages*: repérages, "Entre mer et falaises", n°3, 90/91 . *Le Moniteur architecture AMC*, n° 26, novembre 1991 . Jacques Coulon et Linda Leblanc, *Paysages,* Paris, ed. du Moniteur, coll. Architecture thématique, 1993

Pascal Cribier
Pages paysages: distances, "Le bleu du bleu", n°5, 94/95 . *Pages paysages*: contacts, "Avec vents et marées", n°6, 96/97

Michel Desvigne et Christine Dalnoky
Pierluigi Nicolin (dir. by), *Desvigne and Dalnoky: The Return of the Landscape*/New-York, Whitney Library of Design, 1997

Kathryn Gustafson
Topos European Landscape Magazine, "Der Strand von Le Havre", Munich, n°14, mars 96 . *Kathryn Gustafson*, Spacemaker press, 1997

Laure Quoniam
Connaissance des Arts, "Paysages selon Laure Quoniam", n° 525, fév. 1996 . *D'Architectures*, "la ville côté jardin", n° 65, mai-juin 1996

Alain Richert
Alain Richert, *Parcs et jardins extraordinaires*, Paris, Duchamp-Chevalier

Jacques Simon
Pages paysages: distances, "La campagne dont le paysan est l'auteur est à réinventer", n°5, 94/95 . *Topos European Landscape Magazine*, "Die Straße als Linie, die Landschaft als Schrift", Munich, n°15, juin 96 . "L'art de connaître les arbres", Paris, Hachette, 1964 . "Paysages et formes végétales", ministère de l'équipement et du logement, STU, 1982 . "Jacques Simon, tous azimuts", Paris, Pandora éditions, 1991

Vassivière
Monique Mosser et Philippe Nys (directed by), *Le Jardin, art et lieu de mémoire: colloque de Vassivière en Limousin*, Besançon, éditions de l'Imprimeur, 1995

158

Seine

Ile Saint-Denis
Park

Sausset Park
Aulnay-sous-Bois

Esso Headquarters
Rueil-Malmaison

La Villette
Rue de Meaux

Paris

Jardin
d'acclimatation

André-Citroën Park

The Atlantic
Garden

Garden-City
Plessis-Robinson

Lille

St-Valéry-
en-Caux

Biville
Cherbourg

Le Havre
The Beach

Dieppe

Rouen

Donjon de Vez
Villers-Cotterêts

Normandy

La Coquetterie

Paris

Strasbourg

Seine

Villechétif and Villeroy
Motorway Rest Areas

Troyes

Rennes

Orléans

Chaumont-
sur-Loire

Loire

Burgundy

Blois

Nantes

Dijon

Dole

Urban Park

Desne
Recreational
Zone

Vendée

Issoudun

Parthenay

La Guyonnière
castle garden

Bourg-
en-Bresse

Garden
in the Dombes

Vassivières

Limoges

Lyon

ATLANTIC

Colline de Fourvière

Romans

Imaginary Garden

OCEAN

Bordeaux

Brive-la-Gaillarde

Garden in the Drôme

Aquitaine

Rhône

Garonne

Pont du Gard
Avignon

Toulouse

Nîmes

Provence

Nice

Montpellier

Domain of Le Rayol

Corsica

Marseille

St-Tropez

**MEDITERRANEAN
SEA**

Corsican Garden

Bonifacio

50 km

Cartographie AFDEC

Acknowledgments

The author wishes to thank the landscape architects for their trust and cooperation during the entire period of the investigation, Valérie Brillaud, graduate of the École nationale supérieure du paysage of Versailles, for her information and her critical spirit, and Alain Renouff, in charge of documentation service at the Conservatoire, Chaumont-sur-Loire, for his bibliographical research and his availability.

Photo Credits

Cover: Paul Maurer. P. 2: Deidi von Schaewen.
P. 7: Jean-Baptiste Leroux. P. 8: Arnauld Duboys Freysney (above), doc. Bernard Lassus (below). P. 12: Gérard Dufresne. P. 12: Institut géographique national.
P. 13: doc. Michel Corajoud. P. 14-21: Gérard Dufresne.
P. 22: Arnauld Duboys Freysney. P. 23: doc. Bureau des paysages. P. 24-28: Arnauld Duboys Freysney.
P. 29: Jean-Louis Cohen. P. 30-33: Arnauld Duboys Freysney. P. 34: Gérard Dufresne. P. 35: doc. Jacques Coulon. P. 36-39: Gérard Dufresne. P. 40-51: doc. Sylvie Assassin/Jacques Simon. P. 52, 53: Pascal Cribier.
P. 54: Jean-Baptiste Leroux/Hoa-qui. P. 55-57: Pascal Cribier. P. 58-59: Jean-Baptiste Leroux/Hoa-qui.
P. 60-62: Deidi von Schaewen. P. 63: Pascal Cribier (above), Deidi von Schaewen (below). P. 64: Laurence Toussaint. P. 65: Anna Vivante. P. 66-73: Laurence Toussaint. P. 74-85: Paul Maurer. P. 86: Alexandre Bailhache. P. 87: Ch. Haïssat (above), Alexandre Bailhache (below). P. 88: Alexandre Bailhache (above), Gilles Clément (below). P. 89: Alexandre Bailhache (above), Gilles Clément (below). P. 90: Gilles Clément. P. 91: Gilles Clément (above and below), Alexandre Bailhache (center). P. 92: Deidi von Schaewen. P. 93 Direction des parcs et jardins de la Ville de Paris (map) et Deidi von Schaewen (photo).

P. 94: Alexandre Bailhache. P. 95: Deidi von Schaewen (left), Alexandre Bailhache (right). P. 96-99: Deidi von Schaewen. P. 100: Gilles Clément. P. 101-104: Deidi von Schaewen. P. 105: C. Hopkinson. P 106-109: Deidi von Schaewen. P. 110-111: doc. Kathryn Gustafson.
P. 112: Arnauld Duboys Freysney. P. 114: Gérard Dufresne. P. 115: docs Desvigne-Dalnoky. P 116-121: Gérard Dufresne. P. 122 and 124: Gérard Dufresne. P. 125-127: doc. Brun-Peña. P. 128: Jean-Christophe Ballot.
P. 129: doc. Atelier de paysages. P. 130-133: Jean-Christophe Ballot. P. 134: Franck Lechenet/Altitude. P. 135: Catherine Lambert. P. 136-139: doc. Agence Laure Quoniam.
P. 140: Solaire-Photos (above), Frédéric Magnoux (below).
P.141: Jacques Hoepffner. P. 142 Filipe Martinez.
P. 143-145 Jacques Hoepffner. P. 146: J.-C. Mayer/ G. le Scanff (above), Perdereau (below). P. 147: Chaumont (above). P.148 et 149: J.-C. Mayer/G. le Scanff. P.150: Mosaïk/B. Coutier. P.151: Alain Renouff, J.C. Mayer/ G. le Scanff (left to right), Éric Ossart (above).
P. 152: Keichi Tahara. P. 153: J.-C. Mayer/G. le Scanff. P. 154: Keichi Tahara. P. 155: doc. M. Elsair/J.-P. Delettre. back cover: J.-C. Mayer/G. le Scanff.

Information available (in French) on Education and Training for Landscaping and Related Professions in France

• Formation de paysagiste DPLG: École nationale supérieure du paysage de Versailles (tél.: 01 39 24 62 00) et École d'architecture de Bordeaux (tél.: 05 56 80 65 44).
• Formation d'ingénieur horticole: Institut national d'horticulture d'Angers (tél.: 02 41 22 54 54) et École nationale supérieure de la nature et du paysage de Blois (tél.: 02 54 78 37 00).
• Formation privée: École supérieure d'architecture des jardins à Paris (tél.: 01 43 71 28 53).
• DEA "Gardens, paysage, territoire" à l'École d'architecture de La Villette en collaboration with l'École des hautes études en sciences sociales.
• DESS "Aménagement du paysage" à Aix-Marseille et au CESA de Tours, en collaboration with le Conservatoire des jardins de Chaumont-sur-Loire.
• L'ONISEP a édité deux brochures sur le sujet: "Les métiers de l'agriculture" et "Architectes, paysagistes, urbanistes" (librairie ONISEP, 168, boulevard du Montparnasse, 75014 Paris - tél.: 01 43 35 15 98 ; minitel: 3615 ONISEP).
• Le CIDJ a édité deux fiches, l'une sur les métiers de l'horticulture (n° 2.1441) et l'autre sur les métiers du paysage (n° 2.1442): 105, quai Branly, 75740 Paris cedex 15 - tél.: infos jeunes au 01 44 49 29 30 ; minitel: 3615 CIDJ - et antennes régionales (CIJ).

Printed in Italy by Grafiche Zanini (Bologna).